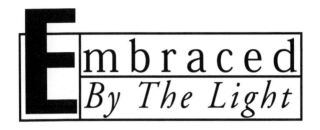

Embraced By The Light

Prayers & Devotions
for
Daily Living

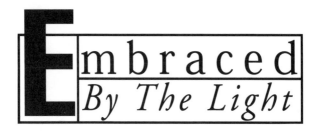

Embraced By The Light

Prayers & Devotions for Daily Living

BETTY J. EADIE

Onjinjinkta Publishing

*Onjinjinkta Publishing*, a division of
Gleska Enterprises
P.O. Box 25490, Seattle, WA. 98125

ISBN: 1-892714-14-0

First Onjinjinkta Publishing hardcover printing
October 2001

Gleska Enterprises.

10 9 8 7 6 5 4 3 2 1

Onjinjinkta is a registered trademark of
Onjinjinkta Enterprises

Printed in the U.S.A.

This Book Is Dedicated to:

God, my Eternal Father,
and Jesus Christ, His Son.
Without their love and sacrifice
I would be lost to fear, guilt,
and shame.

Acknowledgements

I thank my dear readers who suggested I write a devotional with quotes and prayers. Writing it has been a wonderful way for me to internalize the eternal truths taught to me during my near-death experience. I have grown in many ways as a result. And special thanks to the *"Embraced Family."* Your loving presence at the Website, and your encouragement and prayers are greatly appreciated.

To Joe, my children, and the ever-growing number of grandchildren: thank you once more for your love and support. I know deep within my heart that your unusual and independent souls chose to bond with me as family. Your incredible spirit of love blesses our home and lifts me. Your resilience as individuals and family aids me in fulfilling my purpose on Earth.

And special, special, thanks to Stan Zenk, a man of many talents. You are truly a loving friend. Thank you, for sharing those talents, and helping me see this book through. Special thanks to Peter Orullian. While it might have been easier to take a short cut in typesetting, he chose instead to make the most perfect and lovely page. To the rest of my staff at Onjinjinkta Publishing: thank you for your talents and efforts and support. Thank all of you for your patience when I got side tracked and missed deadlines. Thank you for the joy you brought me when you gathered at my home to eat pizza and help scripture hunt. And thank you for helping me deliver this book, one of the finest available!

Author's Note

You belong to a blessed generation of people. Like many, you are opening to God as your Creator and to the inner spiritual powers he has instilled within you. These powers arise from your natural attributes as God's child, and you can learn to use them to improve your life and affect our world for good. Our Heavenly Father is eager to pour blessings upon you of love, understanding, abundance, and joy. These will come as your spirit is ready and able to receive them. If you desire to be better in tune with your inner spirit and with God, this book can be a wonderful tool. It is designed to connect your spirit to knowledge that it is already familiar with, to awaken it to the higher principles learned before coming to earth. Using this book daily with prayer and meditation will develop your spirit, comfort your mind, and add beauty and health to your countenance and body.

Suggestions for Using This Book

This book is best read every day to become a part of your daily habit. Whether you choose the morning, midday, or evening is not important. However, I recommend that you find a time and a place free from interruptions and distractions. You deserve this special time to yourself to balance your busy routine with moments of solitude, introspection, and prayer. This book is designed to be easy to hold and to take with you wherever you go. You may wish to start with the current date or read from the beginning. Or you may want to simply open to a page at random and read, letting the Spirit guide your choice for that day. When you make daily study and prayer your habit, your spirit remains open to God, and he can more readily respond. You will feel his nearness, and you will notice yourself becoming happier, more at peace, more loving, and more confident in facing the challenges of life.

You might choose to share your daily readings with a friend or loved one. If time or situation does not allow for that in person, I have found that sharing over the phone can be fulfilling. Fellowship in study and prayer enhances your spiritual energy and adds strength to your combined prayers.

The Quotations

As you read the quotations, read them purposefully, and contemplate the words. Consider how they might apply to your current circumstances in life. Look for perspectives or principles that are new to you. If a phrase or idea stands out, focus on it, and learn its meaning for you. Should you not understand my perspectives as I have written them here, pray and ask for God's wisdom and understanding. In stillness, open your mind and heart to listen for the inner voice leading you to greater understanding. For further study, you may want to follow the quote's reference to the original book and read more about the topic there. You may also want to look at the index for quotes on similar subjects.

The Bible Verses

In reading the Bible verses, study their connections to the theme for that day. Be open to meanings, which may add new perspective to your traditional Bible learning. After my near-death experience, the Bible became a great lifesaver for me—more so than anyone could imagine. The Bible became my daily breath, my nearness to God, and a touchstone for my soul. Meanings that had been hidden or unclear to me before, suddenly became clear. As I applied what I learned in the spirit world, I felt excitement and surges of energy that held me captive to the Bible. I was amazed that, while I had read the Bible many times from cover to cover, I had never really understood it at all! With the knowledge and understanding that I received in heaven, the Bible came alive to me for the first time. Its writings were more heartfelt, more substantial, and more comprehendible. I could see that I had taken the Bible too literally and without spirit before. I still read and re-read it with delight! I have studied it and underlined so many verses that I had to purchase a new book just for unobstructed reading!

While it is not my purpose or desire to compare *Embraced By The Light* or my other writings to the Bible for scripture comparison, I most assuredly and prayerfully consider the Bible as my second source—next to God and what he has blessed me to experience and to know—as a measuring stick for all that I share. When aligned with his Spirit, I find nothing lacking, and I am at peace.

The Prayers

The prayers I offer here are not intended to be completed prayers. They are a beginning place and suggest, perhaps, where to begin your own prayer for the day. The prayers in this book also add depth to the principles that precede them in the quote and scripture verse. They are purposeful, to bless you with information to meditate on, and to encourage an openness of mind and heart.

I encourage you to pursue your own thoughts, quests, and desires of God. After reading the words of my prayer, continue to pray, adding your own words for as long as the Spirit leads you. I generally close my prayers by saying, "I say these things in the name of Jesus Christ," and then end by saying, "Amen." I do this as an affirmation of my faith and its direction. Let your spirit suggest the appropriate closing for you. The Father already knows what you believe, so choosing your words is more for yourself then it is for him. He listens to your heart. There is no one way to pray, nor is there one way to tell the Father you must close for now.

How you sit, stand or kneel while you pray is a matter of choice and circumstance. You can pray by thought or spoken word. Although, there is added strength in speaking out loud if you are not yet proficient in focusing your thoughts or projecting your energy in them. However, all prayers from the heart are effective. God hears them. There is simply no one perfect way to come to the Father. Just come as you are, invite his Spirit and be open, accepting, and willing to listen to his direction and encouragement for you. You will feel his presence and his love grow in you as you continue to seek him.

The Affirmations

The phrases at the bottom of each page affirm and give positive personal focus. It is best to speak these affirmations out loud, feeling the truth and energy of the words as you repeat them a few times. Memorize those that seem particularly important for you. You may wish to write them and place them where you can read them and be reminded throughout the day. Repetition imbeds these affirming words deep into your spirit and consciousness. They will penetrate to become a part of you, surfacing during moments when you need their strength and reminder.

In heaven I learned that our words create unseen yet very real energies which ripple inward and outward. They carry power to influence and change our environment, our circumstances, our patterns of behavior, our habits of thought, even our very beings. Words spoken in prayer carry these same energies. We are creators, like God is. We are his children and carry within us his attributes. He has created the universe to respond to our words and to support them according to our will. Though God's will is supreme, he allows us the growth experience of using free will to create and influence aspects of our own lives. Speaking inspired words of prayer and affirmation instructs and trains our will, reinforcing us in Godly directions and bringing us closer to alignment with his perfect will.

May God bless you in your daily study and walk with him. May he bless your life with his great wisdom as you continue to learn of him and seek understanding of his will for you.

—Betty J. Eadie

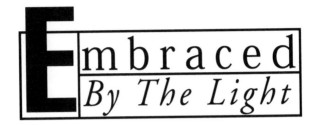

Prayers & Devotions
for
Daily Living

Spiritual Laws
Bless My Life

The knowledge gained from a broken spiritual law can be a gift which eventually blesses many people. But for it to change us, the lesson must be internalized and understood. Then that foundation of understanding can help us to avoid further mistakes and violations of spiritual laws.
The Ripple Effect - page 36

I will never forget thy precepts: for with them thou hast quickened me . . . O how love I thy law! It is my meditation all the day . . . Through thy precepts I get understanding . . . Psalms 119:93-104

Thank you, Father, for the knowledge I have gained from my mistakes. Through them, I can now internalize the importance of your higher laws and come to better understand them and desire to follow them in my life. Forgive me in my ignorance, and bless me with greater wisdom.

Affirmation: **My mind is boundless and free to accept the precepts of God's spiritual laws.**

January 1

Spirit Beings Can Influence Energy

Spiritual beings can inhabit the space around us and share their energy with us. These beings may come from God or Satan, depending on which energy we open ourselves up to. Because like attracts like, a spirit's influence always produces after its kind. *The Ripple Effect - page 73*

Beloved, believe not every spirit, but try the spirits whether they are of God . . . 1 John 4:1

Father, thank you for the knowledge that nothing passes by you without your approval. Without this knowledge, this world with its negative energy would be a frightening place in which to live. I recognize many spirits that are not of you, because they are those which do not include your love. The spirit of anger, lies, contention and fear, are among those easy to recognize. Please bless me to see those which are hidden, and to test them by what they produce. Bless me also to walk in your light, Father, that my spirit may discern your truth in all things.

Affirmation: **I walk in the light of my Heavenly Father, and all is beautiful and good.**

January 2

My Spirit Determines My Actions

We have the ability to determine our own actions. To give in to pride, fear and anger, or to humbly submit to the will of the Spirit, determining to love even when the flesh rebels against it. *The Ripple Effect - page 48*

Ye have been called unto liberty; only use not liberty for an occasion to the flesh, but by love serve one another. Galatians 5:13

Father, thank you for giving me the power to determine the actions of my flesh. Keep my spirit humble and willing to serve you in any capacity that you desire of me. Bless me with a more determined heart that I might always choose what is right. Especially, Father, help me always to choose to love.

Affirmation: **My spirit governs my flesh to follow the path of God in love and in humility.**

God Desires to Bless Me

Gratitude is an eternal virtue. In humility we must ask, and in gratitude we should receive. The more we thank God for the blessings we receive, the more we open the way for further blessings. His desire to bless us is full to overflowing. If we will open our hearts and minds to receive his blessings, we too will be filled to overflowing. *Embraced By The Light - page 107*

It is a good thing to give thanks unto the Lord, and to sing praises unto thy name, O most High: To shew forth thy loving kindness in the morning, and thy faithfulness every night . . . Psalms 92:1-2

Father, thank you for the many blessings that I receive. Help me to express my gratitude not only through my prayers but also by being more responsible for the blessings you grant me. Bless me to use my gifts and talents in helping others, and to demonstrate through physical manifestation my appreciation and love for you.

Affirmation: **I express gratitude to God in prayer and through my love and service for others.**

Understanding Death Creates Well-Being

No emotional trauma distresses us more than the loss of a dear one, and so a proper understanding of death is vital to our emotional and spiritual well-being. Loneliness tests us to the breaking point and can lead us into despair if we let it. However, knowing where a loved one goes after death is important to our healing. It comforts us, as does the knowledge of an eventual reunion on the other side. Loss is natural and important to the growth of our spirits. *The Ripple Effect - page 188*

He healeth the broken in heart, and bindeth up their wounds. Psalms 147:3

Father, thank you for the comforting knowledge that life does not end when I die. And thank you for blessing me with understanding of eternal life, and with knowing that death is but a portal to the spirit world. These truths heal those of us who grieve, and bring comfort and peace to those of us who are dying.

Affirmation: **My loved ones are in the loving arms of God, and I am at peace with the eventual transformation of my own soul.**

Teachers in All Religions

*E*ach of us, I was told, is at a different level of spiritual development and understanding ... All religions upon the earth are necessary because there are people who need what they teach ... Having received this knowledge, I knew that we have no right to criticize any church or religion in any way. They are all precious and important in his sight. Very special people with important missions have been placed in all countries, in all religions, in every station of life, that they might touch others. *Embraced By The Light - page 46*

*F*or whom he did foreknow, he also did predestinate to be conformed to the image of his Son, that he might be the firstborn among many brethren. Moreover whom he did predestinate, them he also called: and whom he called, them he also justified: and whom he justified, them he also glorified. *Romans 8:29-30*

*F*ather, thank you for your personal guidance and for the guidance of those you have chosen to help me find truth. As I find my way, bless me to not offend others who have their own paths to follow. Teach me instead to lend others a hand in seeking you as they must.

Affirmation: **I am eager to find God in my life, and I welcome all teachers blessed to teach me.**

Trials Are a Part of My Growth

$\mathcal{I}$ knew that as part of his plan—as part of our growth—God may allow us to go through trials in a sorting-out period, a cleansing, a purification time when we are often forced to make new decisions based upon our current faith and trust in him.

The Awakening Heart - page 25

The Lord is good, a stronghold in the day of trouble; and he knoweth them that trust in him. Nahum 1:7

Father, every test of my spirit blesses me to see where I am weak and gives me an opportunity to strengthen that area in my life. I am grateful to you for the understanding I gain from challenge, and I need your arms around me, Father, in those times when I don't feel so strong. Comfort my heart with the knowledge that you are with me through each trial. Bless my spirit to recall life in heaven when I was valiant and eager to experience life here even with all its trials.

Affirmation: **I am a valiant spirit chosen by God to experience life here, and I am faithful and eager to continue my journey.**

January 7

My Heart
Communicates with God

Whatever manner in which we choose to communicate with God is not important; these are the mechanical touchstones that we use in our faith, and if we're doing what we think is right, there is a value in that. But what is more important than anything else, ever, is simply that we make that communication with God from the very depths of our heart . . . *The Awakening Heart - page 176*

Then shall ye call upon me, and ye shall go and pray unto me, and I will hearken unto you. And ye shall seek me, and find me, when ye shall search for me with all your heart. Jeremiah 29:12-13

Thank you, Father, for always being there for me when I need you, whether I am on my knees in prayer, in a church, in a temple, or just at a crossroads in my life. When I cry out to you from my heart, you are there. I love you.

Affirmation: **I pray to God with the energy of my heart; and in doing so, I know he hears me.**

Knowledge of Jesus
Fills My Heart

The light that radiated from Jesus was knowledge filled with love, while the dimmer light I had noticed in me was more of a desire for love than love itself. The longer I remained in his presence, however, the brighter my light glowed, absorbing some of his light, which he shared with me. *The Awakening Heart - page 40*

That Christ may dwell in your hearts by faith; that ye, being rooted and grounded in love, may be able to comprehend...the breadth, and length, and depth, and height; And to know the love of Christ, which passeth knowledge, that ye might be filled with all the fullness of God. Ephesians 3:17-19

Father, the more I comprehend what Jesus means to the world, the sweeter his sacrifice is to me. Thank you for his incredible Spirit of Love, and for blessing each person on earth with its power.

Affirmation: **I am blessed with the knowledge that Jesus lives on earth, in heaven, and in my heart.**

January 9

Trials of Faith Teach Patience

Despair is never justified, because it is never needed. We are here to learn, to experiment, and to make mistakes. We don't need to judge ourselves harshly; we just need to take life one step at a time, not worrying about other people's judgment of us, nor measuring ourselves by their measuring sticks. We need to forgive ourselves and be grateful for the things that help us grow. Our most severe challenges will one day reveal themselves to be our greatest teachers. *Embraced By The Light - pages 70-71*

Knowing this, that the trying of your faith worketh patience. But let patience have her perfect work, that ye may be perfect and entire, wanting nothing. *James 1:3-4*

Thank you, Father; though my challenges are often great they have been perfect for bringing me understanding and spiritual growth. My faith and trust in you has blessed me with the ability to forgive myself, and to look only to you as my rod of measurement.

Affirmation: **My greatest trials are also my greatest teachers of faith, forgiveness, compassion and love.**

Jesus Fulfilled
His Mission

I knew that . . . it was necessary for us to experience him, and accept him. As I had looked at Jesus in all his glory, somehow I knew that not only was I accepting of his presence, but I was worthy of him.
The Awakening Heart - page 14

Behold the Lamb of God, which taketh away the sin of the world. John 1:29

Father, there is no greater love than that which Jesus expressed by dying on the cross to save us from our ignorance. His life was sacrificed that we might be saved from the sins of the world by knowing your true nature and will for us. You, Father, are a God of love, patience and forgiveness. Thank you for sending Jesus into the world to remind us of your unconditional love and compassion. Bless me to show my love and appreciation to him by walking in his steps and demonstrating my love for others.

Affirmation: **I walk in the steps of Jesus and demonstrate love, peace, and forbearance.**

January 11

Things of This World
Shall Pass Away

The things of this world matter little to us there—almost not at all. Everything is seen through spiritual eyes. *The Ripple Effect - page 96*

For all that is in the world, the lust of the flesh, and the lust of the eyes, and the pride of life, is not of the Father, but is of the world. And the world passeth away . . . 1 John 2:16-17

Father, I am learning spiritual use for the things of the world you bless me with. And I ask for greater knowledge and greater spiritual abilities to use what I create to bless others who need a touch of heaven. Bless me as I learn to develop my spirit, that I not involve myself emotionally in the things of the flesh. But teach me instead to strengthen my spirit by utilizing what I have to serve you. Thank you for giving me this opportunity to exercise my spirit, by demonstrating my spiritual desires on earth.

Affirmation: **I apply spiritual principles to the things in my life and appreciate the challenge this brings.**

A Home Is Prepared for Me in Heaven

All things have life and glory in heaven, and to describe them in terms of the deadness and stillness of this existence falls short. We will never feel in this life what we will find commonplace forever in our magnificent heavenly home. *The Ripple Effect - page 8*

For now we see through a glass, darkly; but then face to face: now I know in part; but then shall I know even as also I am known. 1 Corinthians 13:12

Father, thank you for the grandeur and magnificence of the earth. You have blessed me to experience its wonder. Because of its beauty, I am in wonderment of the possibilities of heaven. There, I know life truly begins, and there, too, is where the power of your creation is more purely expressed. Thank you for preparing a place for me that is even finer than I am capable of imagining. Bless me to develop my spirit, that I might feel worthy of my home in heaven with you.

Affirmation: **Greater life and beauty awaits me in heaven, and I am worthy of God's generosity and love.**

There Is Power in My Prayers of Faith

Some are given a gift for prayer. Our Creator gave each of us strengths and abilities, and the gift to pray with faith is one of the most powerful. Not all gifts come at birth, however. Many are developed over years if we seek them diligently, asking God to bless us with them. The gift to pray is a gift we might all seek. *The Ripple Effect - page 103*

Wherefore I put thee in remembrance that thou stir up the gift of God, which is in thee . . . 2 Timothy 1:6

Father, thank you for blessing me to seek more spiritual abilities, to grow as you would have me to. Continue to awaken my spirit to the memories of heavenly gifts already instilled in me. Stir up my righteous desires, and bless me to develop my faith more fully and to acquire greater knowledge of you. Bless me also with added strength and power in my prayers and to show my determination as I develop my spirit to its highest potential.

Affirmation: **Through faith, I know God. Through God, I know myself.**

An Exchange of Spiritual Energy Benefits All

Sometimes we take energy, sometimes we give it, which explains why we feel drained or invigorated after interacting with certain people. Sometimes we give and take simultaneously. But rarely does neither happen. Whenever we are near someone, we are either affecting them or being affected by them, usually both. *The Ripple Effect - page 73*

Herefore all things whatsoever ye would that men should do to you, do ye even so to them: for this is the law and the prophets. Matthew 7:12

Father, thank you for blessing my life with the ability to exchange spiritual energy with others. I know now that my desire for others' well being is blessed, not only by my thought, but also literally by my energy which I lend them. I am growing in the wisdom of your laws which govern energies. I know that, while they are inherent within, I must live them outwardly in order to gain greater understanding of them.

Affirmation: **I am a generator of endless love. I access God's love as I share it with others.**

My World Is Blessed with the Glory of God

I was shown that the earth, too, had a spirit life, an energy that God gave it so that it could produce life-giving substances for our benefit. *The Awakening Heart - pages 7-8*

*H*oly, holy, holy, is the Lord of hosts: the whole earth is full of his glory. *Isaiah 6:3*

*F*ather, thank you for blessing the world with your glorious Spirit and for giving it life-supporting elements that provide for my needs. I experience your love daily because I am housed, clothed, and fed by your wisdom, and because you have blessed me to live in a world with natural wonders and beauty.

Affirmation: **The love and glory of God surround and sustain me.**

I Release My Desires to God

I understood that once our prayers of desire have been released, we need to let go of them and trust in the power of God to answer them. He knows our needs at all times and is simply waiting for an invitation to help us. He has all power to answer prayers, but he is bound by his own law and by our wills. We must invite his will to become our own. We must trust him. Once we have asked with sincere desire, doubting nothing, we will receive. *Embraced By The Light - pages 104-05*

Your Father knoweth what things ye have need of, before ye ask him. Matthew 6:8

Father, I invite you into my life and have faith that I will receive your perfect blessings. Bless me with greater desire to come to you in prayer, even while I know you are already aware of my needs. Let me release my desires which can be a burden to me, and gain trust in your greater plan for me. Strengthen my spirit to accept your will, and give me the wisdom to live within it.

Affirmation: **I release my desires to God and trust in his power and wisdom to grant my requests according to his will.**

My Spirit and Body
Seek Balance

Seeking a balance between body and spirit is essential for mortal well-being, as well as for mental and physical health. When I am in this balanced state, my spirit is no longer at the mercy of my body. I was taught in the spirit world that the spirit can control the flesh, raising temporal desires to a higher, more spiritual level . . . It is when we achieve that kind of balance that we function most creatively, spiritually and naturally, while we are here on earth. *The Awakening Heart - page 216*

That the righteousness of the law might be fulfilled in us, who walk not after the flesh, but after the Spirit.
Romans 8:4

Father, thank you for blessing my spirit with the abilities of an earthly body. Teach me to manage the desires of both while I develop Christ-like characteristics by strengthening the love in my soul.

Affirmation: **My Creator knows my spirit and the needs of my body. He blesses them in perfect union.**

There Is Power in Music and in Song

$\mathcal{M}$usic can be a source of great healing—as well as the opposite. Since my return, I had tried to avoid music that takes its listeners to a place of darkness and sought out music that was energized by the power of light and love. *The Awakening Heart - pages 70-71*

When the evil spirit was upon Saul, David took an harp, and played with his hand: so Saul was refreshed, and was well, and the evil spirit departed from him. 1 Samuel 16:23

Father, thank you for gifting me with glorious music to lift my spirit during downcast days. The use of tone for pleasure and for healing is more greatly blessed by your love and felt within us, your children. Bless me to choose music that empowers my soul while bringing a calm and peace to my spirit. And gift me to sing words of praise for all that I am thankful for, especially for you, Father, because you are my song, my melody, my praise and my joy. May you abide in me forever.

Affirmation: **I seek joy and gladness in all things that are praiseworthy and virtuous.**

 January 19

I Blossom as I Internalize God's Will

When I internalized more of my understanding of God's will for me, I felt a sense of freedom and peace that sank deep into me, like a breath of sweet almond blossoms to my soul. My spirit began to swell again as it had when I first recognized the truth and love that existed with God. *The Awakening Heart - pages 42-43*

I delight to do thy will, O my God: yea, thy law is within my heart. Psalms 40:8

Father, thank you for blessing my life with purpose. As I grow to understand you, I learn more of my mission, my purpose for living within your will. Father, I can glory in your plans for me, because I can trust my spirtual growth was motivated by your great love for me and blue-printed by your caring hands. My spirit truly thrills to the fragrance of your spirit and to the life you have created for me.

Affirmation: **My soul thrills to the knowledge of my Creator and the principles of truth he instills in my heart.**

Empathy is
Seeing Ourselves in Others

Negative experiences . . . grant us the power of empathy, to see others as we see ourselves, to comprehend joys and sorrows and all the human impulses. As our eyes are opened and we grow in empathy, our ability to love unconditionally increases. To develop our highest potential, to become like God, we need to gain that which only opposition allows us to gain. *The Ripple Effect - page 82*

For thou, O God, hast proved us: thou hast tried us, as silver is tried...we went through fire and through water: but thou broughtest us out into a wealthy place. Psalms 66:10, 12

Thank you, Father, for urging me beyond sympathy by teaching me the blessings of being empathetic toward others. Knowing others' exact feelings allows me the blessing of truly walking in their shoes and understanding, in a first-hand way, the things that they are experiencing. Thank you for strengthening my spirit with this gift.

Affirmation: **I have greater compassion for others because my Creator gifted me with experience to understand.**

I Am God's Willing Vessel

We are like empty vessels when born: whatever fills us then, is what we later pour.

The Awakening Heart - page 18

And no man putteth new wine into old bottles: else the new wine doth burst the bottles, and the wine is spilled, and the bottles will be marred: but new wine must be put into new bottles. Mark 2:22

Father, bless me to heal from the wounds of my past, and make them less visible to me. I want to feel worthy of your love and capable of being filled with your wisdom. Help me to wipe away all residue of pain and distrust, remembered or those forgotten, so that I might see my spirit renewed by the power of your love for me. Thank you, Father.

Affirmation: **I am restored and ready to serve God in even greater ways than before.**

Growth Comes with a Price and a Reward

*O*ur sufferings come not only with a price, but with a reward. How far will we grow in God's love through the benefit of our trials? Some may be here to break a family's cycle of addiction. Others, to support a family member or friend in their difficult mission. Some come to earth only briefly, but in their few minutes or hours may touch a life for eternity. *The Ripple Effect - page 17*

*B*ut the God of all grace...after that ye have suffered a while, make you perfect, establish, strengthen, settle you. *1 Peter 5:10*

*F*ather, as I grow in spirit, I see your wisdom in allowing suffering to come into lives. Experiencing life's hardships opens the door to greater blessings in our eternal lives. I am learning that all things of greatness come with a price and a reward. Believing this, I am thankful for the loving support of my family and friends as I pass through growing times; for their gifts of love and encouragement; and for the sacrifices they have made for me.

Affirmation: **I give of myself and value the sacrifices made by others.**

 *January 23*

Life Creates Many Points of View

$\mathcal{E}$ach of us develops like a diamond in the rough. The jagged edges are then chipped away and unnecessary roughness removed until we are multifaceted, with many points of view, all the while growing less judgmental and more compassionate from having experienced the pain of living.
The Awakening Heart - pages 24-25

The crooked shall be made straight, and the rough ways shall be made smooth; And all flesh shall see the salvation of God. Luke 3:5

Thank you, Father, for allowing me a spirit that is multifaceted. Its edges, though rough and jagged, will serve you until your Spirit is ready to chip them away. Bless my spirit to hone its already acquired skills and to prepare for life experiences that will bring it to serve an even higher purpose. Thank you, Father, for loving me enough to let me experience suffering, which creates in me the many points of view my spirit requires.

Affirmation: **My Father in Heaven is preparing me to experience the glory that awaits me there.**

I Draw Strength from Like-Minded People

I have also seen the good that religion and churches can bring us. We benefit from gathering in like-minded fellowship with others whose spiritual journeys resemble our own. We draw strength from each other and build strength by sharing the unconditional love of God with each other. And when we assemble in shared spiritual attunement and communicate together with God in prayer, the power of that prayer can be felt by all.

The Awakening Heart - pages 219-220

For where two or three are gathered together in my name, there am I in the midst of them. Matthew 18:20

Father, thank you for the witness that where like energies gather there is greater strength and ability. And, thank you for fulfilling all your promises, that I can trust in and become blessed by the sweetness and strength of those who gather and share in your powerful presence. Thank you for prayer partners, my beloved brothers and sisters in Christ.

Affirmation: **I find joy and strength in uniting myself with others who love and serve the Lord.**

I Am a
Perfect Creation

We . . . bonded together in the spirit world with certain spirit brothers and sisters— those we felt especially close to . . . We understood the influences we would have upon each other in this life and the physical and behavioral attributes we would receive from our families. We were aware of the genetic coding of mortal bodies and the particular physical features we would have. We wanted and needed these. *The Ripple Effect - page 92*

What therefore God hath joined together, let not man put asunder. Mark 10:9

Father, thank you for my genes and for the family that carried them and gifted them to me. Bless me to appreciate all of my attributes, knowing that while sometimes I think I would rather be like somebody else, I know that I am blessed with all that is perfect for me. Bless me to be the very best I can be in all my circumstances.

Affirmation: **All that makes me what I am is perfect for my Creator and his will for me.**

My Spirit Has Ownership of Its Flesh

*E*ach spirit is given ownership of its flesh. While we live in mortality our spirit is to control the body, bringing its appetites and passions into subjection. Everything from within the spirit is manifested in the flesh, but the flesh and attributes of the flesh cannot invade the spirit against the will of the spirit—it is the spirit within us that chooses. It is the spirit which governs.
The Ripple Effect - page 56

*L*ikewise the Spirit also helpeth our infirmities: for we know not what we should pray for as we ought: but the Spirit itself maketh intercession for us with groanings which cannot be uttered. *Romans 8:26*

*F*ather, thank you for hearing the inner pleas of my spirit. My heart cries out for your love and blessings. Bless me to find the most effective balance between my flesh and spirit which promotes health in my body and brings peace and well being to my mind.

Affirmation: **My spirit governs my flesh in a natural balance that manifests outwardly in grace and strength.**

January 27

Sincere Prayers
Produce Miracles

Sincere prayers have power to produce miracles. I have seen many in my life. And I am convinced that countless more occur each day in the lives of those who reach out to God. He answers prayer in his divine voice, in his divine way. If we wait patiently and faithfully, answers will ultimately come. *The Ripple Effect - page 107*

God also bearing them witness, both with signs and wonders, and with divers miracles, and gifts of the Holy Ghost, according to his own will . . . Hebrews 2:4

Father, thank you for the many miracles in my life. And thank you for allowing me to witness answers to my prayers that have blessed me with greater confidence in myself to ask for miracles. Thank you for every miracle I see and for preparing my spirit to accept more miracles as they come. Bless me also to wait patiently with those prayers in my heart that are not ready to be blessed.

Affirmation: **God blesses me to witness many wonders and miracles from heaven.**

I Exist to
Experience Love

As I stood in the presence of Christ he spoke these words: "Above all else, love one another." He was firm, emphatic. This was the most important truth I would learn in my experience with him, and he wanted me to understand it, to feel its full impact. It is the most important thing we can know. To love is the reason we exist.
The Ripple Effect - page 144

And this is his commandment, That we should believe on the name of his Son Jesus Christ, and love one another, as he gave us commandment. 1 John 3:23

Thank you, Father, the impact of your unconditional love for me and for others causes me to realize that I, too, must love as you love. Bless me to become as you are: perfect in the way that you love.

Affirmation: **Every fiber and cell of my being expresses God's reason for my existence: to love.**

I Am
Uniquely Created

$\mathcal{I}$ also understood that sometimes we were given weaknesses which would be for our good. The Lord also gives us gifts and talents according to his will. We should never compare our talents or weaknesses to another's. We each have what we need; we are unique. Equality of spiritual weaknesses or gifts is not important. *Embraced By The Light - page 90*

Be thou partaker of the afflictions of the gospel according to the power of God; who hath saved us, and called us with an holy calling, not according to our works, but according to his own purpose and grace, which was given us in Christ Jesus before the world began. 2 Timothy 1:8-9

Father, in all my strengths and weaknesses I am a tool uniquely crafted by your hands. Use me according to your will.

Affirmation: **I was born to this earth perfectly balanced by God in talents, weaknesses and strengths.**

The Greatest Commandment
Is to Love

If we live true to the spirit we came to earth with, we can progress more quickly. We do that by expressing the love of God that is within us, and we do that by loving God, ourselves, and each other. It is that simple.
The Awakening Heart - page 119

And thou shalt love the Lord thy God with all thy heart, and with all thy soul, and with all thy mind, and with all thy strength . . . And . . . Thou shalt love thy neighbour as thyself. There is none other commandment greater than these. *Mark 12:30-31*

Thank you, Father, for your eternal spirit of love. And thank you for blessing my spirit with opportunities to learn how to love unconditionally. Teach me to express love while I am in the flesh, and keep me always willing to express it, even to those who might be difficult to love. Bless me not to misuse this gift, nor to taint it, but to give it honestly, even through trying times.

Affirmation: **I live true to my inner spirit, and I love and express love honestly and freely.**

January 31

I Am Awakening to My Spiritual Nature

A great Awakening has begun. People around the world are opening their eyes to their own spiritual natures. They are beginning to see who they truly are and what they have always been—beings with an eternal past and a glorious future.
The Ripple Effect - page 14

Awake thou that sleepest, and arise from the dead, and Christ shall give thee light. Ephesians 5:14

Father, thank you for never giving up on me in the many times I attempt to do right, only to fall away from you for lack of understanding. And thank you for gently nudging me awake to my eternal past, which my sleeping spirit only seemed to have forgotten. How great is your love and patience with me. I am aware now of my spiritual nature which longs to be with you always and to feel your glorious love.

Affirmation: **My soul is awakened to my eternal past and glorious future with God.**

My Faith Grows with
Every Answered Prayer

I knew and believed that if I asked for God's will to be done in my life, my prayers would be answered in their time. I began to exercise my faith by prayer, as I had learned, thanking God for all things, no matter how negative they first appeared. *The Awakening Heart - page 25*

And this is the confidence that we have in him, that, if we ask any thing according to his will, he heareth us: And if we know that he hear us, whatsoever we ask, we know that we have the petitions that we desired of him. 1 John 5:14-15

Father, each time I communicate my needs, asking for your will to be done, I am amazed that you answer perfectly and always at the perfect time. I am seeing more clearly now that you answer all my prayers; I simply need to trust your wisdom and timing in answering them.

Affirmation: **My faith in God grows through the exercise of prayer and through His will in my life.**

February 2

God Enlightens and Guides Me

For all of us who listen, in the stillness of our hearts, God enlightens us and offers to lead the way. *The Awakening Heart* - page 12

And thine ears shall hear a word behind thee, saying, This is the way, walk ye in it, when ye turn to the right hand, and when ye turn to the left. *Isaiah 30:21*

Father, your gentle voice is often drowned out by my hectic schedule and by my inability to focus, meditate, and listen for your instructions. Bless me with a spirit of peace and calm because I desire to remain better attuned to your voice, and I thank you for being in my life and offering your direction.

Affirmation: **I listen in the stillness of my heart and hear the sweet voice of God my Creator.**

Jesus Is a Glorious Being

$\mathcal{I}$ would vividly recall each moment spent with Jesus . . . I remembered his incredible countenance, and how powerfully it reminded me that, other than God, my eternal Father, none other was greater than he.
The Awakening Heart - page 14

We beheld his glory, the glory as of the only begotten of the Father, full of grace and truth. John 1:14

Father, thank you for sending Jesus to earth and for blessing me with his perfect example to follow. As I learn to be guided by his light help me to become as he is. Bless me to extend his example by sharing his wisdom and his ways with others.

Affirmation: **I share my wisdom of God like Jesus by following in his ways.**

Heartfelt Prayers Reach Heaven

I saw the sphere of earth rotating in space. I saw many lights shooting up from the earth like beacons. Some were very broad and charged into heaven like broad laser beams. Others resembled the illumination of small pen lights, and some were mere sparks . . . I was told that these beams of power were the prayers of people on earth . . . When we have great need, or when we are praying for other people, the beams project straight from us and are immediately visible. *Embraced By The Light - page 103-104*

Their prayer came up to his holy dwelling place, even unto heaven. 2 Chronicles 30:27

Father, thank you for listening as I pray for myself and for others. Bless me to convey my desires more clearly to you in prayer, to make my requests simple and focused and full of loving energy. May I always remember to say, "Thank you," because showing my appreciation is a part of showing my love for you.

Affirmation: **I pray simple, heartfelt prayers that project powerfully into heaven.**

The Art to Loving Can Be Acquired

I began to practice giving love, at first sending it out by thought to people whom I wanted to love, then actually expressing it to them. Soon the art of loving became one of my greatest strengths . . . I didn't acquire the ability to love from just my own efforts; rather, I opened myself up to its possibility and it began to come to me from others.
The Awakening Heart - page 40

God loveth a cheerful giver. And God is able to make all grace abound toward you; that ye, always having all sufficiency in all things, may abound to every good work . . . 2 *Corinthians* 9:7-8

Father, I am learning that there is an art to loving others, especially those who have been wounded by love and no longer trust it. Help me to continue being open and giving while others learn that love can be a beautiful exchange. Bless me with every loving attribute pleasing to you, that I may bring joy and give comfort whenever these are needed. By every act and deed, let me witness of your love.

Affirmation: **I am blessed sufficiently in serving God, and he gives me greater work to do.**

Angels Are Near, Anxious to Assist

I saw that we all volunteered for our positions and stations in the world, and that each of us is receiving more help than we know. I saw the unconditional love of God, beyond any earthly love, radiating from him to all his children. I saw the angels standing near us, waiting to assist us, rejoicing in our accomplishments and joys. *Embraced By The Light - page 53*

I will lift up mine eyes unto the hills, from whence cometh my help. My help cometh from the Lord, which made heaven and earth. *Psalms 121:1-2*

Thank you, Father, for blessing me with life on earth. I know that through my experience your purposes are served, and my joy is in doing your will. Bless me to see and appreciate your sustaining efforts in my struggles. And let me feel your Spirit and the presence of the angels who wait to assist me.

Affirmation: **Angels assist me in my life's journey on earth.**

My Thoughts Possess
Power to Create

From our thoughts, seeds are produced. By the use of our tongue, our word, we plant them. By our deeds, we nurture them.
The Awakening Heart - page 214

For as he thinketh in his heart, so is he. Proverbs 23:7

Father, keep my thoughts kind and prayerful, and teach me to hold my tongue except to glorify you. Keep me focused on loving others and expressing that love through appreciation. Bless me to use every creative power to bless and to help others. Make my voice strong in praise of you and able to awaken strong desires in others to know you and love you. And bless me to use the strength of my daily prayers to make an eternal difference by the power of my being.

Affirmation: **My life naturally aligns with God's will as I create goodness by my thoughts, words and actions.**

The Kingdom of God
Is Within Me

Our love on earth is not as pure or fully developed as God's love. But each time I recalled his love, the memory of it flowed through me again . . . Our oneness, the part of us that is love, is in our cellular memory; it is present in all of us. It is the single most healing energy we have. *The Awakening Heart* - page 41

For, behold, the kingdom of God is within you.
Luke 17:21

Father, it is difficult to understand that any part of my mortal being is pure enough to be your kingdom or dwelling place. Bless me, Father, to see the simplest truth that you are love, and that the kingdom is my soul.

Affirmation: **I am a being of love, and all that I desire is love.**

Steadfast Prayer
Keeps Me Focused

The dilemma of unanswered prayers is as old as mankind. Job, in his affliction, sought God day and night, wondering if the Almighty had forsaken him. He had lost his children, his wealth, his reputation, and his health. Painful boils covered his body. His wife and friends told him to repent of imaginary sins, then finally to curse God and die. In desperation, Job sought God even more urgently. His constant efforts kept him focused on God. *The Ripple Effect - page 100*

For I said in my haste, I am cut off from before thine eyes: nevertheless thou heardest the voice of my supplications when I cried unto thee. Psalms 31:22

Thank you, Father, I know you hear my every prayer, from the softest whisper of my heart to the most urgent cry of my soul. I also know that you answer every prayer, even though, sometimes, I do not see or hear the answer. Bless me to be steadfast in prayer and remain as open to you as you are to me.

Affirmation: **I am steadfast in prayer and focused on God and his will for my life.**

February 10

I Envision Christ's Love Around Me

When I pray, I envision the energy and love of Christ surrounding me. I allow myself to bask in his glow, even if the glow is at first only created in my mind. Our thoughts have great power to create results, and visualizing God is one way to exercise faith in him . . . Christ can feel so near to us in prayer that sometimes we can almost touch him. At these times, the act of praying becomes almost a revelation in itself. Visualizing may even turn to vision. *The Ripple Effect - page 106*

That the God of our Lord Jesus Christ, the Father of glory, may give unto you the spirit of wisdom and revelation in the knowledge of him: The eyes of your understanding being enlightened . . . Ephesians 1:17-18

Father, thank you for continuing to reveal Christ to me. Bless me with the ability to feel his nearness. Help me use the creative power of my thoughts in wisdom and in knowledge of you, so that I might be drawn closer.

Affirmation: **I visualize the face of Christ, and see the wisdom and glory of God.**

February 11

In Heaven Are Degrees of Glory

I learned that different levels or degrees of glory exist in heaven. Some spirits appear brighter and more glorious than others, yet it is important to note that no spirit judges another because of station or degree of growth. Individuals are who they are, and they are accepted and loved completely, regardless of personal development. *The Ripple Effect - page 8*

There is one glory of the sun, and another glory of the moon, and another glory of the stars: for one star differeth from another star in glory. 1 Corinthians 15:41

Father, I accept the glory within me, for I know that I am as I have grown to become. Bless me, as I continue to develop, to reach my fullest potential, that I may be as you created me and desire me to become.

Affirmation: **The love within me radiates in my countenance, expressing the great spirit I am.**

My Eternal Foundation Is Family

*L*oving families lay the foundation for our eternal progress. They help us build strength, identify and overcome weaknesses, and bring challenges of their own for us to overcome. They significantly influence us in our earthly missions and affect how we influence others in their missions. Every family bond . . . can play a crucial role in teaching us how to love and be loved. *The Ripple Effect - pages 187-188*

*A*nd he left the oxen, and ran after Elijah, and said, Let me, I pray thee, kiss my father and my mother, and then I will follow thee . . . *1 Kings 19:20*

*F*ather, thank you for the love I receive from my family and friends. And thank you for the reassurance that the challenges they bring me can also bless if I choose to use them that way. Help me to support my loved ones in their earthly missions, even as they provide the experiences I need to accomplish mine.

Affirmation: **I acknowledge that earthly bonds fulfill heavenly promises, and I am grateful for the family God has given me.**

February 13

When Receptive and Flexible, My Spirit Grows

The spirit, not unlike the human mind, must be receptive and flexible in order to expand and develop as I did. I never thought that I had either of these qualities, but I could accept the fact that all things are possible through God. *The Awakening Heart - page 16*

I will run the way of thy commandments, when thou shalt enlarge my heart. *Psalms 119:32*

Father, thank you for giving me unlimited potential and a mind and spirit designed to continually expand. Bless me not to fall into rigid tradition, but rather to be flexible and open, and to have as much faith in myself as you have in me. Help me follow my intuition, trusting it to lead me to you.

Affirmation: **I embrace inspiration and change, and my receptiveness is used by God.**

My Heartfelt Desires
Generate Energy

*O*ur passion is the energy through which we serve our purpose. When we serve our purpose, we feel our passion. By following our passion, we will tap into the energy God gives us to serve our purpose.
The Awakening Heart - page 223

*H*ope deferred maketh the heart sick: but when the desire cometh, it is a tree of life. *Proverbs 13:12*

*F*ather, thank you for creating passion in me and for allowing this drive to bless my life with the energy needed to fulfill my purpose. Bless me, Father, with your direction in all things, even in the desires of my heart. Let my passions not feed my ego, but rather, let them serve your purposes.

*A*ffirmation:　**The desires of my heart are aligned with God, and I am fulfilling my mission and purpose.**

Religion Can Point to God, But I Must Find Him

Religion can point us to God, but religion does not keep him. Even if we are active in a church and a congregation, we must find our Heavenly Father individually, each for ourselves. *The Ripple Effect - page 116*

Behold, I stand at the door, and knock: if any man hear my voice, and open the door, I will come in to him, and will sup with him, and he with me. Revelation 3:20

Father, thank you for gracing my life with your Holy Presence and for filling my heart with your love. Thank you for each opportunity to learn of you, for each experience which causes me to seek after you. Help me accept responsibility for my own growth, my own daily walk with you.

Affirmation: **I seek God daily and find him in my heart.**

Prophetic Dreams Prepare Me for Things to Come

Dreams of prophecy draw directly upon the foreknowledge of God. They serve a number of purposes, preparing us for events to come, offering hope, and giving direction. Many of the ancient prophets took great hope in their dreams and visions of Christ, both of his mortal ministry and of his advent in the last days. Today, many prophetic dreams and premonitions tell of trials to come and warn us to prepare ourselves temporally and spiritually for the future. *The Ripple Effect - page 137*

And it shall come to pass in the last days, saith God, I will pour out my Spirit upon all flesh: and your sons and your daughters shall prophesy, and your young men shall see visions, and your old men shall dream dreams . . . Acts 2:17

Father, thank you for opening my spirit to your truths during sleep, when my senses are less in tune with the world. In your wisdom, this connection helps me prepare and accept trials that must come, and helps me to know that my life is on course.

Affirmation: **Through my visions and dreams, God clearly directs and instructs me.**

February 17

My Deeds Create Endless Ripples

The Savior stepped toward me, full of concern and love. His spirit gave me strength, and he said that I was judging myself too critically. "You're being too harsh on yourself," he said. Then he showed me the reverse side of the ripple effect. I saw myself perform an act of kindness, just a simple act of unselfishness, and I saw the ripples go out again. The friend I had been kind to was kind in turn to one of her friends, and the chain repeated itself. I saw love and happiness increase in others' lives because of that one simple act on my part.
Embraced By The Light - pages 113-114

Now he that ministereth seed to the sower both minister bread for your food, and multiply your seed sown, and increase the fruits of your righteousness . . . 2 Corinthians 9:10

Father, thank you for the understanding that all of your children are connected to each other. Bless me with self-awareness and self-discipline so that everything I do will create positive ripples.

Affirmation: **Every day I start new ripples of thoughtfulness, kindness and love.**

February 18

The Spirit World Is
Dynamic and Joyful

I understood that there is a vital, dynamic link between the spirit world and mortality, and that we need the spirits on the other side for our progression. I also saw that they are very happy to assist us in any way they can.
Embraced By The Light - page 48

There is joy in the presence of the angels of God . . .
Luke 15:10

Thank you, Father, for the assistance from those in the Spirit World who are dynamically linked to my spiritual development. Bless me to feel their joy when I am successful and to follow their guidance should my challenges move me off course.

Affirmation: **Heavenly beings encourage me and take joy in my progression.**

My Soul Waits to Be Prompted by God

I could now see that God was teaching me how to be patient and wait on him. Trusting him, believing in him, and knowing that he really is in control, I knew he will give us, his beloved children, the righteous desires of our hearts when we ask for them. *The Awakening Heart - page 25*

My soul, wait thou only upon God; for my expectation is from him. *Psalms 62:5*

Father, thank you for being patient with me as I grow in my belief and trust in you. Bless me with righteous desires to live my life according to your will, and teach me patience in waiting for your perfect timing in all things.

Affirmation: **God's control in my life blesses me, and I seek only his will to be done.**

My Lord's Humor
Is Delightful

I'll never forget the Lord's sense of humor, which was as delightful and quick as any here—far more so. Nobody could out-do his humor. He is filled with perfect happiness, perfect goodwill. There is a softness and grace in his presence, and I had no doubt that he is a perfect man. *Embraced By The Light - pages 72-73*

*A*nd the Lord their God shall save them in that day as the flock of his people . . . For how great is his goodness, and how great is his beauty! *Zechariah 9:16-17*

*F*ather, my spirit rejoices when I experience kindness and love in humor. Thank you for giving me joy and laughter. Bless me to live more joyously and to find happiness in my relationships with others.

Affirmation: **Perfect happiness, joy and kindness are expressed in my Christ-like humor.**

My Spirit Body Is Perfect and Whole

My new body was weightless and extremely mobile, and I was fascinated by my new state of being. Although I had felt pain from the surgery only moments before, I now felt no discomfort at all. I was whole in every way—perfect. And I thought, "This is who I really am." *Embraced By The Light - page 30*

For we know that if our earthly . . . tabernacle were dissolved, we have a building of God, an house not made with hands, eternal in the heavens. For in this we groan . . . knowing that, whilst we are at home in the body, we are absent from the Lord . . . We are . . . willing rather to be absent from the body, and to be present with the Lord. 2 Corinthians 5:1-8

Thank you, Heavenly Father, for providing both flesh and spirit. Keep me mindful to respect both temples, both bodies, because doing so glorifies you and perfects me.

Affirmation: **In all things I praise the Father and accept who I really am in him.**

Our Return to God Is Pain-and Sorrow-Free

*K*nowing the truth surrounding death liberates us from fears which can hinder our progression. Sometimes we are concerned that a loved one suffered or was afraid at the end. We may feel guilty because of our helplessness in preventing the death or the suffering. But grief and guilt are alleviated by knowing that suffering is part of our plan and that God does not let us endure more pain than our spirits can withstand. When we reach the other side we will learn that each death experience is an important factor in our spiritual development. *The Ripple Effect - pages 188-189*

*A*nd God shall wipe away all tears from their eyes; and there shall be no more death, neither sorrow, nor crying, neither shall there be any more pain: for the former things are passed away. *Revelation 21:4*

*F*ather, how wonderful it is to know that I need not fear death! Thank you for your promise to be with me in the hour of my passing, and thank you for bringing me Home when my time is through.

Affirmation: **I rejoice in the knowledge that life is eternal with God.**

February 23

I Am Patterned after God with Many Talents

God created us like himself and gave us gifts, special talents to develop and to use as we chose. He is the pattern that we are to follow, and his example would be the greatest respect to the earth that so richly gives of all it has. *The Awakening Heart - page 9*

Every good gift and every perfect gift is from above, and cometh down from the Father of lights, with whom is no variableness, neither shadow of turning. James 1:17

Father, thank you for my special gifts and talents that, by design, draw me to a clearer understanding of you. Teach me to use them with perfect love as you do, and bless me to remain open to receive more abilities as I perfect those which I already have.

Affirmation: **God created me and patterned me after himself. I am a co-creator with him.**

Heavenly Father Is
Generous in His Care

*G*od never punishes us by taking the life of one we love. He never lets a child die because he does not care. God cares more, and is more aware, that we suspect . . . Our children are always before our Father in Heaven, always in his grace, always in his generous care. *The Ripple Effect - page 62*

*A*re not two sparrows sold for a farthing? And one of them shall not fall on the ground without your Father. But the very hairs of your head are all numbered. Fear ye not therefore, ye are of more value than many sparrows. *Matthew 10:29-31*

*D*ear God, you are such a perfect, loving father! Thank you for watching over my loved ones, which I know you do, even in those moments when things seem out of control. Help me to be comforted in times of trial, confident that nothing escapes your notice and loving care.

Affirmation: **I live each day with the peace of God in my heart, knowing that my Heavenly Father cares.**

In Understanding God My Confidence Increases

Having faith in God and in his plan for us implies that we don't weaken ourselves or others through chronic anxiety. We must trust that he is aware of our situations, trust that if we have made mistakes, he is able to bless us to do better now and in the future.
The Ripple Effect - page 78

According to the eternal purpose which he purposed in Christ Jesus our Lord: In whom we have boldness and access with confidence by the faith of him.
Ephesians 3:11-12

Father, my anxiety fades when I remember that nothing passes by you without your divine approval. Thank you for tenderly watching over me and for protecting me from things I cannot control. Bless me to have confidence in myself as I learn to become more like you.

Affirmation: **I acknowledge the power of God in me and boldly express that confidence.**

My Mission and Purpose
Will Be Done

Gently, he opened his arms and let me stand back far enough to look into his eyes, and he said, "Your death was premature, it is not yet your time." No words ever spoken have penetrated me more than these . . . I felt a mission, a purpose; I didn't know what it was, but I knew that my life on earth had not been meaningless. It was not yet my time. My time would come when my mission, my purpose, my meaning in this life was accomplished. I had a reason for existing on earth. *Embraced By The Light - pages 42-43*

To every thing there is a season, and a time to every purpose under the heaven: A time to be born, and a time to die; a time to plant, and a time to pluck up that which is planted . . . Ecclesiastes 3:1-2

Father, give me courage, strength and pa-tience to wait for your perfect timing in all things. I trust in your full view of my life from your first creating of me to the eternities yet to come. And only your sight and fore-knowledge is pure.

Affirmation: **My reason for being is fulfilled in God's perfect timing.**

I Learn Through Free Will

*F*reedom of choice is precious, and our individual agency may be the most precious gift we have from God next to life itself . . . In heaven, free will was gifted to all who would come here, and we willingly accepted it for ourselves and granted it to others. We desired it as a responsibility and a challenge for our lives on earth. We asked God for the right to make mistakes, even to sin or to break spiritual laws so that we might learn. We desired to live with the consequences of our mistakes so that we could be driven from within to revise our lives. *The Ripple Effect - pages 41, 43*

It is good for me that I have been afflicted; that I might learn thy statutes. Psalms 119:71

Father, in your wisdom you endowed me with everything I need to make the most of this life, including free will. Thank you for my freedom and for the responsibility that comes with it. Help me use it wisely. Bless me with the patience and love I need to respect the choices of others.

Affirmation: **I am conscious of the power God has given me in free will, and I use it for his glory.**

I Am Responsible for
My Health

I had learned each of us is responsible for our body while on earth, that it is up to us to tap into the power within us that affects the health of our body, mind, and spirit and important to bring the three into harmony.

The Awakening Heart - page 32

I wish above all things that thou mayest prosper and be in health, even as thy soul prospereth. 3 John 1:2

Father, I am grateful for my physical body that was created perfectly for me. Through your understanding of me and my purpose on earth, you blessed my spirit with the flesh best suited for its growth. Bless me to become a worthy caretaker of it, to be moderate in all things. Teach me to keep both spirit and flesh in harmony. Help me make time each week for a day of rest and reflection that will keep my spirit in tune with your loving Spirit. Thank you, Father, for the opportunity to prove your trust in me as I exercise the power of self-control.

Affirmation: **I maintain power and control over my mind, body, and spirit. I am strong, healthy, and balanced in all that I do.**

God Judges the
Heart's Intent

*A*fter the death of our body, we have a life's review where . . . we don't just watch our lives. We experience the effects that our actions have had on others . . . The life review is an important part of our spiritual growth.
The Awakening Heart - page 118

*A*nd I saw the dead, small and great, stand before God; and the books were opened: and another book was opened, which is the book of life: and the dead were judged out of those things which were written in the books, according to their works. *Revelation 20:12*

*F*ather, keep me aware of my daily actions and mindful that each act creates a ripple in another's life that will eventually return for me to learn by. Create in me a new heart incapable of hurting anyone for any reason, but full of only good desires for all. And bless me to desire only good.

*A*ffirmation: **My heart's intent is to serve in endless love for all people.**

Friends Are My Earth Angels

We may become like the angels themselves, helping others who are in need. In prayer and service our lights will always shine. Service is the oil to our lamps generated by compassion and love. *Embraced By The Light - page 107*

He that loveth his brother abideth in the light, and there is none occasion of stumbling in him . . . *1 John 2:10*

Father, may I be a port in the storm, a lighthouse by the sea, a secret blessing to my friends or to anyone else who needs my support. Bless me to "be there" for them when I am needed, and insightful enough to "back off" when I am not.

Affirmation: **Compassion flows from me through service for others, and I bless the lives of my friends as heavenly angels do.**

I Test My Limits to Grow in Confidence

We live and thrive by doing things, by testing our limits, by opening ourselves up to new experiences and challenges, by seeking joy and even happiness as we step out—not in fear or anxiety, but in faith. *The Ripple Effect page 78*

Be not afraid of sudden fear, neither of the desolation of the wicked, when it cometh. For the Lord shall be thy confidence, and shall keep thy foot from being taken. Proverbs 3:25-26

Father, I realize that at times I have slowed my spiritual growth by being afraid of new ideas or ways of doing things. With your help, I will be open to each new divine inspiration, and I will go boldly and confidently where my heart leads. I know that, if I follow the path with you as my guide, nothing can harm me or stand in my way.

Affirmation: **I live each day with confidence and courage, pushing beyond perceived limits in my constant quest of spiritual gain.**

The Power of Heaven
Is Love

God wants us to draw on the powers of heaven, and if we are attuned, we will recognize when we have a chance to tap into the energy he has provided for us or to be of service when our own energy can help accomplish his will. Our strength, like our good deeds, sets the ripple into motion. It is the sacred sharing of love that keeps us going. *The Awakening Heart - page 103*

My flesh and my heart faileth: but God is the strength of my heart, and my portion for ever. *Psalms 73:26*

Father, as I learn to emulate you, I will serve with all my energy and share with others the love you so freely bestow upon me. I recognize that, after all I can do, there is yet more I can accomplish with your divine help. Thank you, Father.

Affirmation: **I am capable of greatness because the source of my strength is love.**

Ministering Angels Surround Me

*T*hree men suddenly appeared at my side. They wore beautiful, light brown robes, and . . . a kind of glow emanated from them. I sensed in them great spirituality, knowledge, and wisdom . . . And I knew that these were my choicest friends in that greater life and that they had chosen to be with me. They explained that they, with others, had been my guardian angels during my life on earth. But I felt these three were special, that they were also my "ministering angels."
Embraced By The Light - pages 30-32

*A*re they not all ministering spirits, sent forth to minister for them who shall be heirs of salvation?
Hebrews 1:14

*F*ather, often I have felt so alone. During grievous times I have wept, longing for a companionship that only my spirit comprehends. I am beginning to know that what I yearn for is your presence, because nothing else satisfies. Thank you for loving me, and for sending ministering angels to comfort me.

Affirmation: **I am surrounded by loving arms that embrace me in my sorrow. Ministering Angels soothe my spirit and calm my aching heart.**

March 5

My Faith Includes the Mysteries of God

*E*ach child has a mission to fulfill before dying. We will always miss our departed children, but we can rejoice in the knowledge that their missions were successfully completed. And we can be comforted with the certainty that the child is free from the pain and troubles of this world and is joyful in the loving arms of God. *The Ripple Effect - page 66*

*S*uffer the little children to come onto me, and forbid them not: for of such is the kingdom of God. *Mark 10:14*

*F*ather, thank you for caring for me through the times when I can not see the entire image of what you have planned for my life. Help me find comfort with the knowledge that some spirits need only be here a short time while others must linger. Help me to rejoice in the successful completion of each person's mission, and help me to honor the memory of those who have passed by keeping the ripples of their love alive.

Affirmation: **My faith includes the mysteries of God, and they enrich my life.**

March 6

God Is a
Compassionate Father

God perfectly understands our lack of knowledge. He knows that most of us do not remember our commitments to him. In his eyes we are like little children: susceptible and even expected to make mistakes.
The Ripple Effect - page 38

The Lord is good to all: and his tender mercies are over all his works. *Psalms 145:9*

Thank you, Father, for in your wisdom I learn to live by faith without perfect knowledge. This, I know, refines my spirit, as you know my weaknesses and frailties. In my ignorance I often fall like a baby learning to walk. But I know that you are always beside me, lifting me and holding me. Your grace and love offer me hope through the tender mercies of Jesus Christ, who set the path and directs me to walk in his light.

Affirmation: **My Heavenly Father loves and understands me. He forgives me with endless compassion.**

March 7

I Am Becoming a Light unto Others

*A*s we each find one person with whom to share our light, a wonderful miracle begins to take place; we find the Lord answering our individual prayers and preparing us to become the light, the answer, to yet many others. *The Ripple Effect - page xvi*

*A*rise, shine; for thy light is come, and the glory of the Lord is risen upon thee. *Isaiah 60:1*

*F*ather, I am so grateful for the blessings of light and love in my life. The peace and calm I feel carry me through the day. May I learn to share my own light as freely as you have done with me, by showing concern for others, giving as charitably as I am able, and speaking of your goodness when the spirit directs me to do so.

Affirmation: **I am a spirit of light and love, and I share these qualities liberally.**

Developing a Harvest of Faith

Developing faith is like planting seeds. Even if some of our seeds fall by the wayside, we will still receive some harvest. Any act of faith will bless us. The more proficient we become (and we will become more proficient if we practice), the greater our harvest of faith will be. Everything produces after its own kind. *Embraced By The Light - pages 65-66*

But this I say, He which soweth sparingly shall reap also sparingly; and he which soweth bountifully shall reap also bountifully. 2 Corinthians 9:6

Father, thank you for blessing me to develop my faith and for teaching me that, as I use what I have, I will acquire more. Bless me with freedom from self-doubt that I might explore that what has been unreachable in my life. Most of all, Father, bless me that the fruits of my labor be harvested in heaven. Keep me exploring my faith in you and sowing seeds of faith in others.

Affirmation: **I plant seeds of faith in others, and my goal for spiritual harvest is sure.**

My Friendships Magnify Every Good Thing

*A*nything wonderful is made more so if you can share it, and I now wanted to share the knowledge that I had received and to learn more about the beliefs of others. I knew that strength could be found among like-minded people . . . *The Awakening Heart - page 41*

*I*f we walk in the light, as he is in the light, we have fellowship one with another, and the blood of Jesus Christ his Son cleanseth us from all sin. *1 John 1:7*

*F*ather, bless me with like-minded friends that I may open my heart, and exchange knowledge and wisdom with them. Keep me always willing to include others and to use my strengths to bless their lives.

Affirmation: **I choose friends who bring me strength and joy, whose qualities magnify my life.**

Jesus Is
Whole and Perfect

*H*e was Jesus . . . I knew that he had the ability to appear to me or others in more than one way . . . however it was necessary for us to experience him and accept him . . . Jesus, I "knew," need never show me the nail prints in his hands nor the gash in his side as proof of who he was. I belonged to him just as I was, and the fact that he had suffered pain was not the issue now. *The Awakening Heart - page 14*

Though he were a Son, yet learned he obedience by the things which he suffered; And being made perfect, he became the author of eternal salvation unto all them that obey him . . . Hebrews 5:8-9

Father, thank you for your Son, Jesus Christ. Through his sufferings he was made perfect and is the example I wish to follow. Bless me to more fully understand his purpose, to trust that, through following him, I will be drawn closer to you.

Affirmation: **I follow Jesus' living example of perfection, truth and love.**

March 11

My Mind Is Open to the Riches of Heaven

When we are able to expand our minds and hearts to accept the riches of heaven, we will receive them. This is our Creator's promise to us. To accept, we must open. To gain more, we must share. *The Ripple Effect - page 9*

Make me to understand the way of thy precepts: so shall I talk of thy wondrous works. *Psalms 119:27*

Father, you are always ready to bless me in more ways than I can imagine. Help me overcome all limiting thoughts, all feelings of unworthiness, all doubts and fears so that I may open myself to the multifaceted prosperity you desire to give me. Help me also to be a responsible steward. May the ripples of your blessings never end at me but continue on to bless the lives of countless others. Thank you, Father, for you unending generosity!

Affirmation: **I gratefully accept the knowledge, experience, health, wealth and unconditional love the Creator sends me.**

Jesus Delights
in Me

As more questions bubbled out of me, I became aware of his sense of humor. Almost laughing, he suggested that I slow down, that I could know all I desired. *Embraced By The Light - page 44*

Delight thyself also in the Lord; and he shall give thee the desires of thine heart. *Psalms 37:4*

Thank you, Father, for creating me to love deeply and to have joy. You have blessed me with so many wonderful ways to express myself; through humor, laughter, song and dance. I am indeed created in your likeness. In all my ways may I reflect your beauty, goodness and love, bringing endless delight to your heart.

Affirmation: **My spirit delights in the ways of my Lord, and he delights in me.**

My Faith Can Move Mountains

*F*aith opens us to new and sometimes wonderfully crazy ideas. Why? Because in faith, we believe that God—in his strength and good grace—will show us when we go too far, and that if we get hurt, he will help us to learn from the experience. God sends blessings that will amaze us when we trust in his power to bless. *The Ripple Effect - pages 78-79*

*J*esus answered and said unto them, Verily I say unto you, If ye have faith, and doubt not, ye shall not only do this which is done to the fig tree, but also if ye shall say unto this mountain, Be thou removed, and be thou cast into the sea; it shall be done. *Matthew 21:21*

*F*ather, when I doubt, I never doubt you or your abilities. I desire the same freedom from doubting myself. Help me to trust my strengths and feelings. Bless me to remove by faith the shadowy mountains and dark valleys in my life. Help me cast out all fear and doubt by blessing those things in the past which I have cursed through faltering faith.

*A*ffirmation: **I trust in the power of God to bless me in strength and confidence.**

March 14

God Possesses All Truth

One of the grandest mysteries of God is his foreknowledge. Truth is knowledge of things as they were, as they are, and as they are to come. God, possessing all truth, has the ability to know all things in advance. This being the case, we can trust him to give us only that which will be good for us in completing our life's mission successfully.
The Ripple Effect - page 125

Trust in the Lord with all thine heart; and lean not unto thine own understanding. In all thy ways acknowledge him, and he shall direct thy paths.
Proverbs 3:5-6

Father, even as I am limited in my understanding, I recognize your supreme knowledge and see the wisdom in trusting your plan for me. I am at peace submitting my will to your eternal truth, which will bring about goodness and honor in my life's course.

Affirmation: **I trust God knowing his every action is guided by truth.**

Adversity Is Common to Mankind

The challenges are high for this life. They are nothing less than completing our journeys on earth and learning to love as God loves in eternity. Forgiveness is understanding, and to understand is to grow. Each soul is ultimately responsible for his or her own happiness and for the success or failure of his or her earthly mission. All have trials and tribulations to overcome. *The Ripple Effect - page 59*

There hath no temptation taken you but such as is common to man: but God is faithful, who will not suffer you to be tempted above that ye are able; but will with the temptation also make a way to escape, that ye may be able to bear it. 1 Corinthians 10:13

Father, in growing to become like you, I know I must stand against the hardships of this life. Bless me with patience to understand the adversity I encounter. Give me a forgiving heart so that I may respond to difficulties with honor, and from them find happiness.

Affirmation: **I find joy in forgiving others, and I accept responsibility for my own happiness.**

Spiritual Laws
Bless and Protect Me

We are like babies crawling around, trying to learn how to use the forces within us. They are powerful forces and are governed by laws that will protect us from ourselves. But as we grow and seek the positive all around us, even the laws themselves will be revealed. We will be given all that we are prepared to receive. *Embraced By The Light - page 71*

For precept must be upon precept, precept upon precept; line upon line, line upon line; here a little, and there a little . . . Isaiah 28:10

Father, thank you for organizing the forces that govern, teach, and bless me. Help me to see that my life, while unlimited by restraints, is governed by laws that protect and bless me. Teach me to live within your spiritual laws, to understand them and to use them when I have grown in wisdom.

Affirmation: **I am open to all positive forces within and around me.**

Heaven Communicates Through Dreams and Visions

There exists a spiritual veil which blocks us from God and his mysteries. While we dream, the veil thins and partially lifts . . . God communicates with us through dreams . . . in order to send messages and reminders meant to further us in our life's missions . . . We can never predict when they will come, but if we believe and are open to them, they will come. *The Ripple Effect - page 139*

In a dream, in a vision of the night, when deep sleep falleth upon men, in slumberings upon the bed; Then he openeth the ears of men, and sealeth their instruction . . . Job 33:15-16

Thank you, Father, for leading the way as I strive to complete my earthly mission. It is comforting to know that even when I sleep you are reaching out to me, blessing me with needed guidance. Bless my ability to recognize those dreams which are actually a lifting of the veil. Help me to interpret the personal symbols in my dreams, to understand them clearly.

Affirmation: **I am blessed with dreams and visions and have wisdom to understand them.**

March 18

I Invite God's Spirit to Instruct Me

Through prayer we are reminded of who we are, where we are going, and what God would have us do. By listening to God's answers to our prayers, we learn the language of the Spirit, which is so important for us to learn. But before we can listen, we must invite. *The Ripple Effect - page 96*

He that received seed into the good ground is he that heareth the word, and understandeth it . . .
Matthew 13:23

Thank you, Father, for bringing me to surrender to your wisdom. Instruct me in aligning my heart and actions with you always. Teach me to walk constantly with the Spirit as I seek to follow after you. And bless me to listen to the still, small voice inside me, and to live so that it may always burn within.

Affirmation: **I invite the guidance of my Father and am prepared in heart and mind to receive and live it.**

Experience Is My Greatest Teacher

*A*ll of my experiences now took on new meaning. I realized that no real mistakes had been made in my life. Each experience was a tool for me to grow by. Every unhappy experience had allowed me to obtain greater understanding about myself. *Embraced By The Light - pages 114-115*

I have learned by experience that the Lord hath blessed me . . . Genesis 30:27

Father, thank you for forgiving all my unwise choices in life. Help me also to forgive myself. I recognize that when you gave me free will and sent me to this world with its many possibilities, you knew I would stumble at times or go off course. Thank you for never giving up on me, even when I am tempted to give up on myself. And thank you for turning even my poorest choices into opportunities for spiritual growth.

Affirmation: **Every experience brings me enlightenment and spiritual growth.**

Missions in Life Have
Blueprints in Heaven

*I*n the pre-mortal world we knew about and even chose our missions in life . . . our stations in life are based upon the objectives of those missions. Through divine knowledge we knew what many of our tests and experiences would be, and we prepared accordingly . . . We came as volunteers, each eager to learn and experience all that God had created for us. *Embraced By The Light - pages 48-49*

*A*ll things work together for good to them that love God, to them who are the called according to his purpose. *Romans 8:28*

*T*hank you, Father, for guiding me back when I stray from the mission you chose for me. Thank you for blessing me with the strength and fortitude as I struggle to endure life to its end.

Affirmation: **My life is laid out by my Creator, and my spirit follows his perfect plan.**

It is My Life's Purpose to Love and Serve God

I was shown that we each have a purpose . . . But I do not believe that it is important for us to know God's purpose for our lives. He knows, so we don't have to; we are only here to serve. It is less important that we know our purpose than that we serve it well. And he gives us what we need to do that.
The Awakening Heart - page 223

If ye shall hearken diligently unto my commandments which I command you this day, to love the Lord your God, and to serve him with all your heart and with all your soul . . . I will give you the rain of your land in his due season . . . *Deuteronomy 11:13-14*

Father, thank you for blessing me with a purpose. Though I do not understand my purpose completely, I seek to follow your commandments and do as you request of me. I will follow your will by honoring and serving even as Jesus did. Through my efforts, Father, bless me to draw nearer to you and to fulfill my purpose according to your will.

Affirmation: **I have reason to live abundantly, and through my unreserved efforts I serve the Lord, my God.**

My Attitude Affects My Relationship with God

Nothing comes between us and God's love except what we place there. Our self-righteousness and judgmental attitudes often mask the obstacles we've created that block us from God's love. *The Awakening Heart - page 42*

Keep yourselves in the love of God, looking for the mercy of our Lord Jesus . . . Jude 1:21

Father, when I feel distance between us, I know it is not you moving away, but me, because of my thoughts or actions which I feel do not serve you. Forgive me for this, and help me to rid myself of that which I allow to come between you and me. Thank you, Father, for your patience. Bless me to accept that you are loving me even as I learn.

Affirmation: **My relationship with God is not based upon my failures, but upon my love.**

My Life's Ripple Effect
Reaches Countless Souls

I knew that reaching even just one soul with the message of God's love would set in motion a reaction that passed that hopeful message to others and then more, rippling out to reach countless souls. *The Awakening Heart - page 4*

So by the obedience of one shall many be made righteous. *Romans 5:19*

Father, bless me with determination to be a loving example to others. Increase my willingness to share the happiness I have come to know with all who would receive it. Let me feel the depth of concern and love that may forever change the hearts of those I seek to pass your message to. And thank you, Father, for blessing my life with the ripples of love that I receive from others.

Affirmation: **I am a willing messenger whose love and concern ripples into many lives.**

As I Pray, I Grow in Patience and Faith

I continued my prayers to God, despite the feeling that I received no answers. *The Awakening Heart - page 30*

And he spake a parable unto them to this end, that men ought always to pray, and not to faint . . . Luke 18:1

Father, thank you for blessing me with the scripture that I should pray and not faint. It has blessed me to have patience and not give up. At times I reach out to you but feel unheard and without your presence. Yet I know you are with me always and hear all my prayers, so I know you never abandon me. Your love and perfect timing in answering my prayers strengthens my patience and teaches me to wait upon you in faith.

Affirmation: **I wait upon God who is always available to me and whose timing is always perfect.**

We Are Taught of God to Love One Another

*R*emember, in everything we do—including righting an injustice or preventing a wrong—we are to love. It is our purpose on earth to learn to love as Jesus loves . . .
The Ripple Effect - page 43

*B*ut as touching brotherly love ye need not that I write unto you: for ye yourselves are taught of God to love one another. *1 Thessalonians 4:9*

*F*ather, though my soul recalls your heavenly love, the earthly part of me sometimes forgets to love my fellow man. Thank you for forgiving this in me. Deepen my knowledge that I must share love in order to grow, and strengthen my capacity to love when I find it most difficult.

Affirmation: **I am created from love, therefore loving is natural for me.**

Problems Are My Golden Opportunities

There is no escaping our problems . . . because they arise from the needs of our spirit. Our "problems" are actually gifts. They are opportunities for us to understand and to overcome the weaknesses in our souls . . . We should view each problem as a tool for refining and furthering our growth. In doing this, we embrace life to its fullest. *The Ripple Effect - pages 205, 206*

Behold, I have refined thee, but not with silver; I have chosen thee in the furnace of affliction. Isaiah 48:10

Father, at times my life seems so complicated and difficult to manage that I feel I could not handle one more problem. In such moments, help me to remember that there is a divine purpose for everything, and that if I run away from problems, they will only return later as even greater challenges. Bless me with courage to face them, and the wisdom to recognize and embrace the lessons they bring me.

Affirmation: **I face each problem with a prayerful heart and willingness to grow.**

March 27

My Thoughts Create
My Reality

During my experience, I had learned that our thoughts create our lives. *The Awakening Heart - page 30*

Commit thy work unto the Lord, and thy thoughts shall be established. Proverbs 16:3

Thank you, Father, for creating me with the power to establish my own life and to live it according to my own creative mind. Bless me to design and commit my work to glorify you and fulfill your will for me. Bring to my thoughts and actions the desire also to create a loving environment for my family and friends.

Affirmation: **My thoughts create a life which God uses to advance his kingdom on earth.**

God Blesses Me with
Boundless Love and Knowledge

Unconditional love and knowledge have no boundaries; there is no "how," "who," "if," or "when." I had feasted at Jesus' feet and experienced the boundless, unconditional love of my creator, my God. Knowledge was poured into me unconditionally, and the joy that brought was beyond compare.
The Awakening Heart - page 43

O the depth of the riches both of the wisdom and knowledge of God! *Romans 11:33*

Father, you are Unconditional Love and are therefore boundless in your grace and mercy, love and joy. Your will and your purpose for me is to become just as you are: limitless in love. Thank you for blessing me with this truth which sets me free from the boundaries established by the ignorance of mankind.

Affirmation: **Truth and love are limitless in God, and I take joy in accepting myself as limitless as well.**

March 29

God's Love Is
Pure and Everlasting

*L*ove is an emotion of energy that unless expressed, remains unseen. It has power to change the universe. It is endless, it never dies. It cannot hurt, it cannot possess, it cannot withhold. God is Love. He created us in his image. And we have the power in the flesh to express love for God, love for self, and love for all humankind.
The Ripple Effect - page 159

The Lord hath appeared of old unto me, saying, Yea, I have loved thee with an everlasting love: therefore with loving kindness have I drawn thee. Jeremiah 31:3

Thank you, Father, because I am your child and can walk in this confidence through every day of my life. I can live in the joy of being an expression of you and in carrying within me your loving Spirit. Bless me to share this holy part of myself with others. May I always express to you my deepest love and gratitude.

Affirmation: **As an expression of God, I love others with purity of heart.**

This World Is Not My Natural Home

Coming back from the spirit world gave me a new awareness of this world. It changed not only the way I saw the world, but the way I saw myself. The things that I had once desired for my family and for myself were no longer so appealing. I used to long for material things, and I had sacrificed for many of them. But now I could see how easy it is to get caught up in materialism—and how it can hold us back from our spiritual focus!
The Awakening Heart - page 17

Love not the world, neither the things that are in the world. If any man love the world, the love of the Father is not in him. 1 John 2:15

Thank you, Father, I appreciate the world you created for my education. I am drawn to its miracles and beauties. So bless me to find the appropriate balance of living here, and loving here, while keeping in my heart a yearning to be with you.

Affirmation: **My greatest joy is in my Creator and in the heavenly home he holds waiting for me.**

God's Angels
Are at Work on Earth

God gives us signs of his will for us. Many of our experiences are orchestrated by his guardian angels. They walk among us in greater numbers than we know, and they help provide us with the opportunities we need to progress in our spiritual growth. We can see their hand in daily life, though we may dismiss their deeds as coincidence. When we are in tune with God's will, we can see these coincidences as what they are: our windows into the divine. *The Awakening Heart - pages 224-223*

And he dreamed, and behold a ladder set up on the earth, and the top of it reached to heaven: and behold the angels of God ascending and descending on it. Genesis 28:12

Father, to claim coincidence when miracles happen in life is not to see your angels at work here on earth. Thank you for the miracles that have blessed me and for the unseen hands of angels who guide me.

Affirmation: **My daily life is orchestrated by God, and being in tune with him offers windows of opportunities.**

April 1

The Spirit of Fear Is Not Given by God

We have the power to exercise faith in God and in his plan for us. We have the power to grow in confidence of our ability to meet problems head on. And in doing these things we develop power to transform our fears of life into love of life. *The Ripple Effect - page 80*

For God hath not given us the spirit of fear; but of power, and of love, and of a sound mind. 2 Timothy 1:7

Father, thank you for blessing me with power and love and a sound mind. Bless me to use these attributes to solve my problems and not put things off because I lack confidence in getting them done. Bless me also to remember that nothing passes by you without your approval. Knowing this, I can deal with whatever comes up, having enthusiasm within and the expectation of serving you. Thank you for bringing me to see the things in my life which I need change.

Affirmation: **Through the power of God, I meet my problems head on.**

Christ Would Neither Say Nor Do Anything to Offend

I developed a relationship and knowledge of the Savior that I will always cherish. His concern for my feelings was inspiring; he never wanted to do or say anything that would offend me. *Embraced By The Light - page 72*

*R*emember, O Lord, thy tender mercies and thy loving kindnesses; for they have been ever of old. *Psalms 25:6*

*F*ather, thank you for blessing my life with Jesus. His expression of love is what I choose to follow and emulate in every way I can. He is truly divine, Father, for in his willingness to show his love through sacrifice, he is the exact expression of you. Like you, he personifies tenderness, mercy and kindness. Bless me in my growth to be kind, to never offend, and teach me to convey your goodness in my every expression.

Affirmation: **Because I emulate the characteristics of Jesus, I am tender, loving, and kind.**

The Energy of My Love Brings Joy

Love is really the only thing that matters, and love is joy . . . It all seemed so simple. If we're kind, we'll have joy. *Embraced By The Light - page 114*

These things have I spoken unto you . . . that your joy might be full. This is my commandment, That ye love one another, as I have loved you. John 15:11-12

Father, teach me patience, tolerance and compassion so that I can love more purely. Bless me with the gift to forgive others and to respond to them with a loving heart. Help me to bring the very best of me into my relationships and to let joy be the expression of my loving energy. Thank you, Father, for showing me by example that perfect love brings perfect joy.

Affirmation: **I love as the Heavenly Father loves, and his love brings joy to my life.**

The Creator Does
Not Afflict

God never uses his love to hurt us. To do so would countermand his own law of judgment. "Do unto others as you would have them do unto you," Christ said in Matthew 7:12. So he will never let us down, will never forsake us. His love is extended to all, and he knows exactly how to reach each person . . . *The Ripple Effect - page 54*

Touching the Almighty . . . he is excellent in power, and in judgment, and in plenty of justice: he will not afflict. Job 37:23

Thank you, Father, for bringing me love and expressing it through your kindness and tolerance. Thank you, too, for witnessing to the world through Jesus, that you are not a God who afflicts, but a God of love. Your judgment allows pain for a pivotal point of growth, but you are always there to lend your hand and blessing to see me through.

Affirmation: **God is my source of love, abundance, and change.**

Visions and Dreams Unite
Heaven and Earth

The Creator uses time to bring forth truth in a season when the meaning may carry more significance for us. Experiencing truth in dreams and visions leads to greater acknowledgment of them and therefore greater acceptance. This openness, in turn, allows for other similar experiences which can then lead us to total enlightenment.
The Ripple Effect - page 143

For the vision is yet for an appointed time, but at the end it shall speak . . . though it tarry, wait for it; because it will surely come . . . Habakkuk 2:3

Father, thank you for dreams that bless me while I sleep and for insights that come in visions while I am awake. I open myself to the many ways you reveal truth to me. During those special moments, help me discern your voice and will, and quicken my mind and spirit to learn so I can grow toward complete understanding.

Affirmation: **My spirit is quickened by the Lord and invites his will into my conscious and subconscious mind.**

Blessed with Free Will, I Act for Myself

We were given agency to act for ourselves here. Our own actions determine the course of our lives, and we can alter or redirect our lives at any time . . . We were grateful for this ability to express our free will and to exercise its power. This would allow each of us to obtain great joy or to choose that which will bring us sadness. *The Ripple Effect - page 49*

I the Lord search the heart . . . to give every man according to his ways, and according to the fruit of his doings. Jeremiah 17:10

Father, I am like a child who is becoming aware of the cause and effect of its actions. Please hold my hand tightly as I walk through life, and though I must experiment to learn on my own, guide and direct me, and keep me from harm while I grow.

Affirmation: **I acknowledge my gift of free will to choose, and I choose to walk in the will of my Creator.**

God Has Power to Answer All Prayers

God has the power to listen to and answer all prayers at all times. To pray to him sincerely is not to trouble him, but to trust him, and he will respond to our trust. *The Ripple Effect - page 96*

How excellent is thy loving kindness, O God! Therefore the children of men put their trust under the shadow of thy wings. Psalms 36:7

Father, nothing I ask for is beyond your power to grant should it be your will to do so. You consider all my requests and in your limitless power and wisdom, you answer each one according to your perfect timing and will. Thank you, Father. Your constant care is wonderful to me.

Affirmation: **My trust in God includes his power to answer all my prayers.**

April 8

I Hold the Keys of Heaven's Gate

We hold the keys to prison's door and heaven's gate. When will we choose to learn within the perfect love and light of God? As soon as we do, we throw off our shackles of fear and guilt. By turning the key to heaven, by desiring to enter therein, we allow our Savior to reach us, to save us, to teach us how to become more like him. *The Ripple Effect - page 124*

Shew me thy ways, O Lord; teach me thy paths. Lead me in thy truth, and teach me: for thou art the God of my salvation; on thee do I wait all the day. Psalms 25:4-5

Father, thank you for gifting me with keys that open doors to opportunity and growth. Help me especially to keep open the door to your love and truth so that fear and guilt and false tradition don't blind me to your ways. Fill me, Father, with courage and conviction to find and follow the true path to heaven's gate, that I might enter and dwell with you forever.

Affirmation: **I desire to learn of God and to follow the path of my Savior to heaven.**

April 9

As I Learn,
Doors of Opportunity Open

In reviewing my life I saw that I often repeated the same mistakes, committing the same harmful actions over and over, until finally I learned the lesson. But I also saw that the more I learned, the more doors of opportunity were opened to me. And they were literally opened. Many things I thought I had done by myself were shown to have been extended by divine help. *Embraced By The Light - page 115*

I know thy works: behold, I have set before thee an open door, and no man can shut it: for thou hast a little strength, and hath kept my word, and hast not denied my name. Revelation 3:8

Thank you, Father, for the amazing way you open doors for me once I am ready to go through them. Your love for me flows into every area of my life, encouraging me and giving me confidence. Bless me with the wisdom to see every opportunity as an open door, and bless me to step through them without hesitation.

Affirmation: **God opens doors of opportunity and I walk through with eagerness and gratitude.**

April 10

I Seek First the Kingdom of God

I began to speak, and as I started sharing my experience, I felt a hush of peace surround me. I knew that I was doing what I was supposed to do, and that God was caring for my other concerns while he used me here.
The Awakening Heart - page 72

Therefore take not thought . . . what to eat . . . what to drink . . . for your heavenly Father knoweth that ye have need of all these things . . . but seek ye first the kingdom of God, and his righteousness; and all these things shall be added unto you. Matthew 6:31-33

Father, thank you, for the awesome power of your love that supplies all my needs. Forgive me each time I feel alone in my efforts, each time I doubted your concern and care for me. Hindsight and experience show me that you are always with me, teaching me, guiding me, loving me. Bless me in my faith until I know without doubting that you are by my side. Let me never hesitate along my path to growth.

Affirmation: **When I seek God I find Him, loving me, caring for me, and blessing me.**

April 11

God's Wisdom Is Perfect in All Things

$\mathcal{A}$lthough we may sense a greater or lesser development in people, we are not to speculate on their final judgment. Only God knows where we will be happiest. In his wisdom he will ensure us the opportunities to experience and enjoy all that is possible—which is far beyond what anyone can imagine for themselves. *The Ripple Effect - page 10*

Eye hath not seen, nor ear heard, neither have entered into the heart of man, the things which God hath prepared for them that love him. 1 Corinthians 2:9

Father, bless me to resist the urge to judge others, to place them above or below me in spiritual development. Help me to remember that each person's journey is his own, that glorious rewards await all of us in returning home to your love.

Affirmation: **I allow each person his place along the path of growth, seeking only to love him as God does.**

True Love Creates
Happiness and Peace

If we love God enough to follow his teachings, we will be able to differentiate between love and false love in others. We will love all people with a Christ-like love, the kind that helps others without being seduced by them. This pure, tough love is kind and patient, but it is also protective and honest. It does not allow us to grovel. If we have love for self, we will do things which lead to happiness, which give us light, and which bring peace into our lives. *The Ripple Effect - page 154*

That your love may abound yet more and more in knowledge and in all judgment . . . Philippians 1:9

Thank you, Father. Each type of love I experience on earth prepares me for that which is pure and sweet in heaven. Help me recognize the selfishness in man's interpretation of love compared to yours, Father, which asks nothing in return and is unconditionally given.

Affirmation: **I seek Christ-like love which I know to be pure, honest and never-ending.**

The Lord Guides
My Earthly Journey

*M*y life since my return from the spirit world had been a difficult journey of awakening, a journey that I knew would continue to unfold in years ahead. I had not brought myself here: I had only followed.
The Awakening Heart - page 11

I am the Lord thy God . . . which leadeth thee by the way that thou shouldest go. *Isaiah 48:17*

*F*ather, thank you for directing my path and blessing me with insight along the way. Forgive me when in my eagerness to make plans, I fail to seek your direction, forgetting your promises to guide me. Bless me with the certainty of your will for my life, and remind me to leave behind the pride of my own understanding and trust in you.

Affirmation: **I trust God's direction, and I follow it in obedience to his will.**

I Have Power Over Illness and Disease

$\mathcal{I}$ began to see . . . many of my own weaknesses and recognized that I had the ability to overcome my own creations . . . I could deny . . . illnesses the power to express themselves in me. *The Awakening Heart - page 32*

For if ye live after the flesh, ye shall die: but if ye through the Spirit do mortify the deeds of the body, ye shall live. Romans 8:13

Father, when my body hurts or functions improperly, I can easily forget that I am much more that a physical being. Bless me with self-awareness to identify the underlying spiritual or emotional problem that is manifesting itself as physical illness. Help me overcome it with courage, and faith, and an attitude which invites your healing into my life. Then help me avoid further illness by guarding my thoughts, feelings, words and actions against all negativity. Thank you, Father, for blessing me.

Affirmation: **I invite positive energy into my life, and my physical and emotional health are increasing in response.**

My Children Are
Treasured Beings

I saw my children running up and down the stairs and knew . . . they were individual spirits, like myself, with an intelligence that was developed before their lives on earth . . . I knew that my children had their own life agendas and that when they had completed them, they too would end their stay on earth . . . There was no need for sorrow or fear. In the end each of my children would be all right, and I knew that it would be only a brief moment before we were all together again.
Embraced By The Light - pages 34-35

Train up a child in the way he should go: and when he is old, he will not depart from it. Proverbs 22:6

Blessed Father, my joy is complete in my children. Bless them when I am both near and far from them. They are my treasured gifts from heaven. Thank you, Father, for blessing me through parenthood to know unconditional love.

Affirmation: **God sanctions my role as parent, and I bear my responsibility well for his divine children.**

April 16

I Am a
Light unto Others

Now I no longer desired conversion for anyone. I saw that they must desire change for themselves, and I knew that God, our loving Father, would place that in their heart when or if they were ready. *The Awakening Heart - page 43*

Ye are the light of the world. A city that is set on an hill cannot be hid. Neither do men light a candle, and put it under a bushel, but on a candlestick; and it giveth light unto all that are in the house. Let your light so shine before men, that they may see your good works, and glorify your Father which is in heaven. Matthew 5:14-16

Father, bless me to demonstrate my religious belief outwardly through Christ-like ways, free of judgment and force. Keep me mindful that knowledge of you is dead in me until it is revealed by my acts. Bless truth to be alive in me, Father, and let me bear witness of you. And thank you, Father, for gifting me with light and blessing me to share it with my spiritual brothers and sisters.

Affirmation: **As an example to others, I radiate love and acceptance.**

My Spirit Is Free to Choose My Religion

Religion is a personal matter. One's religion, one's faith and beliefs may be influenced by, or even dictated by, a church or other individuals . . . Each individual spirit claims the freedom to believe for himself. If we were to analyze each person's deepest beliefs— including assumptions, guesses and hopes— we would never find two people who believe exactly the same thing, even with the same religion. *The Ripple Effect - page 108*

For we must all appear before the judgment seat of Christ; that every one may receive the things done in his body, according to that he hath done, whether it be good or bad. 2 Corinthians 5:10

Father, thank you for blessing my life with religions that have offered me experience in finding you. Without a starting point in my life, I might not have thought to learn more. Your blessings have brought me further along, and I know that I will continue to grow in your love.

Affirmation: **I follow my heart, and it leads me back to my Creator.**

April 18

I Seek Within My Soul the Love of God

On earth our spirits miss the electrifying power of God's love. Our minds are veiled, but our spirits remember his love, and silently we cry for its comfort and soothing warmth. Some of us spend our lives weaving in and out of relationships, searching for the essence of this divine emotion, hunting it, craving it, but never finding it in this world. Some of us cry to God for this love, expecting him to send it to us through another person. But it first must come from ourselves . . . *The Ripple Effect - pages 145-146*

O God . . . my soul thirsteth for thee, my flesh longeth for thee in a dry and thirsty land, where no water is . . . Because thy loving kindness is better than life, my lips shall praise thee. Psalms 63:1,3

Father, I hunger for the exchange of love so common in heaven. My heart is bursting with that love, and my soul cries out to express it. Let me experience more to learn of its power and joy, then teach me to share it appropriately with others.

Affirmation: **I recognize the power of God's love within me, and I express that love openly and freely.**

April 19

Heaven Is Beautiful
Beyond Description

As we went outdoors into the garden I saw mountains, spectacular valleys, and rivers . . . The garden was filled with trees and flowers and plants that somehow made their setting seem inevitable, as if they were meant to be exactly how and where they were. I walked on the grass for a time. It was crisp, cool, and brilliant green, and it felt alive under my feet . . . A beautiful river ran through the garden . . . and I was immediately drawn to it . . . The water dazzled with its clarity and life. *Embraced By The Light - pages 78-80*

But there the glorious Lord will be unto us a place of broad rivers and streams . . . *Isaiah 33:21*

Father, thank you for fashioning earth after heaven. To see its most beautiful parts is to glimpse the shadow of my heavenly home. Your powers as my Creator are beyond comprehension, and I am in awe and wonder of what awaits me in heaven.

Affirmation: **My eyes are open to the reflection of heaven's beauty all around me.**

My Abilities Are
Gifted by the Creator

Our individual missions were assigned according to the talents and abilities God gave us at our creation. In performing our missions we magnify our talents beyond their original capacity. The Father wants all his offspring to expand their talents that they might grow in spiritual abundance, have a more perfect joy, and glorify him more completely. *The Ripple Effect - pages 10-11*

A man can receive nothing, except it be given him from heaven. John 3:27

Thank you, Father, for gifting me with talents and abilities in greater abundance than I know. Bless me to identify them, and to magnify them to their highest potential. Then help me to use them to glorify you by opening me to your will.

Affirmation: **I use my talents and abilities in service to magnify my God.**

God's Love Ripples Through Me to Others

When God compels us and offers opportunities for teaching his love and truth, we must teach as Christ taught: meekly, lovingly, and by laying down our convenience and temporal security. Then, like so many dominoes set up by his hand, we touch our neighbor, we unite as one, and God's love and truth ripple out into all the world. *The Ripple Effect - page 44*

As every man hath received the gift, even so minister the same one to another, as good stewards of the manifold grace of God. 1 Peter 4:10

Heavenly Father, open my eyes to the needs of others, and help me minister to them as Jesus would. Bless me with his sacrificial love, that I may put aside my own comforts and serve willingly, that his life may live on in me.

Affirmation: **I live after Christ and express his attributes of humility and grace.**

God Holds My Will
Sacred and Pure

We come to mortality with a mission in life and with our days known and agreed to. However, our free will is held sacred and inviolate. God will guide us, but he will never force us to follow the plan we agreed to. The choice is in our hands to pursue life to its natural end or to sever it prematurely. We should never consider suicide as part of God's plan for anyone. *The Ripple Effect - page 203*

What man is he that desireth life, and loveth many days, that he may see good? Psalms 34:12

Father, my days on this earth are blessed, numbered, and counted by you, and they are perfect for my spiritual growth. Thank you for them. Bless me with awareness that the purpose for my life is to expand my intelligence, to grow through understanding the effects of my choices. Bless me to pursue life diligently without fear of the unknown and to never give up when I am challenged.

Affirmation: **My life is sanctioned by God, and I choose to pursue it with all its challenges.**

Love Returns Me to Heavenly Father

$\mathcal{W}$hen [Jesus] came he taught us about God's pure love. And his demonstration of that love was when he laid down his life for us. It was part of his mission, part of the entire plan for mankind. We may not understand completely all that he did or why he did it, but I know with certainty that through his example of love, as he demonstrated it, is the way back to light and truth, the way back to Heavenly Father.
The Ripple Effect - page 31

$\mathcal{F}$or even hereunto were ye called: because Christ also suffered for us, leaving us an example, that ye should follow his steps . . . 1 Peter 2:21

$\mathcal{F}$ather, the magnetism of your love attracts its likeness with intensity. The more I release love to others, the more my love grows, and the more I feel drawn to you. Make clear my understanding as you bless me to love as you love, with fullness of heart.

$\mathcal{A}$ffirmation: **I live the example of Jesus Christ by loving unconditionally.**

April 24

My Needs Are Defined When I Pray

God is approachable . . . [and] wants us to have things, both spiritual and material things. Nothing is wrong with asking for what you need. And you can be as specific as you need to be. God wants that. It is good to define what your needs are . . . God knows our needs before we pray about them, but he wants us to know and understand them. *The Awakening Heart - pages 224-225*

Thou shalt make thy prayer unto him, and he shall hear thee . . . Thou shalt also decree a thing, and it shall be established unto thee: and the light shall shine upon thy ways. Job 22:27-28

Father, thank you for leading me to the desires within my heart. And thank you, too, for not always filling my desires when what I asked for would not truly bless me. Teach me to weigh my needs and to seek only those things which bring me closer to the Spirit.

Affirmation: **I identify my needs and seek those which bless me.**

To Be Spiritually Minded Is Life and Peace

I saw how damaging lust for the things of this world can be. All real growth occurs spiritually, and worldly things like possessions and rampant appetites smother the spirit. They become our gods, binding us to the flesh, and we are not free to experience the growth and joy that God desires for us.
Embraced By The Light - page 117

For they that are after the flesh do mind the things of the flesh; but they that are after the Spirit the things of the Spirit. For to be carnally minded is death: but to be spiritually minded is life and peace.
Romans 8:5-6

Thank you, Father, for blessing me to be spiritually minded and to seek after life which is with you. Teach me to use my knowledge of the Spirit's ways in order to gain greater understanding of you. The more I know of you, the more I know of my own true nature, Father, because you created me like you . . . for which I thank you.

Affirmation: **I am growing in the joy of my Creator, and seek life with Him that brings peace.**

Earth Is a School for Spiritual Development

I was actually relieved to find that the earth is not our natural home, that we did not originate here. I was gratified to see that the earth is only a temporary place . . . *Embraced By The Light - pages 49-50*

For what is your life? It is even a vapour, that appeareth for a little time, and then vanisheth away. James 4:14

Heavenly Father, thank you for creating a place where my spirit can develop by experiencing life in the flesh. This education is important to my spirit's continuing effort to become more like you. Little children remind me how I once was. They lack knowledge as I did, but will learn and develop in remarkable ways as life's experiences expand them. Might I always remember that you see me as a child, too, Father, full of endless potential for growth in this life and in the eternities.

Affirmation: **I am a child of God, learning to become as he is: wisdom and love.**

Above All Else, I Am to Love

The details of my experience are important only to the point that they help us to love. All else is an appendage to that. It is simply a matter of following the Savior's message which he most clearly expressed to me: "Above all else, love one another."
Embraced By The Light - page 147

For this is the message that ye heard from the beginning, that we should love one another. 1 John 3:11

Father, bless me to know the spiritual law that governs giving and receiving. As I love you, your spirit is free to flow into mine. As I love myself, I expand and have more love to give. In giving love, I open myself to receiving even greater love from you. Stretch my ability to love, Father, by blessing me to give it fearlessly and selflessly.

Affirmation: **My priorities are in order: First I love God, then I love myself, now I am capable of loving others.**

April 28

I Fellowship with
My Lord

Though at times I feel profoundly alone on my journey, I know that he is leading others, too, and that our sharing of his message of love is part of his plan. *The Awakening Heart - page 11*

That which we have seen and heard declare we unto you, that ye also may have fellowship with us: and truly our fellowship is with the Father, and with his Son Jesus Christ. 1 John 1:3

Thank you, Father, for never leaving me alone as I serve you. The presence of your sweet spirit fills the void I often feel in my heart. Bless me with the fellowship of others, and keep me directed to find peace in you.

Affirmation: **I am never alone in the work of the Lord, for he is with me always.**

Spoken Words Create
Lasting Vibrations

I saw different energies surround different people. I saw how a person's words actually affect the energy field around him. The very words themselves—the vibrations in the air—attract one type of energy or another . . . If we understood the awesome power of our words, we would prefer silence to almost anything negative. In our thoughts and words we create our own weaknesses and our own strengths. *Embraced By The Light - page 58*

But I say unto you, That every idle word that men shall speak, they shall give account thereof in the day of judgment. *Matthew 12:36*

Father, forgive me for not realizing that, as your child, I too have the power to create by my spoken words. Give me greater understanding of that power and its uses for good. Bless me to guard my words against negativity, to bless all things as you do rather than to curse. Increase my ability to dispel darkness and evil in the world by speaking words of light and life.

Affirmation: **I speak positive words which attract positive energies and create inner strengths.**

April 30

Love with Family and Friends Is Eternal

Our bonds with loved ones continue after death as they began long before birth. The love between us is eternal and does not cease simply because we cannot see the departed. Those who have passed to the other side are very much alive—more so than ever—and they are able to comfort us and send us their love. But they are also bound by laws which govern our lives and which limit their free contact with us. Yes, they care about us, about our lives and our welfare, but they must not interfere with our progression in life. *The Ripple Effect - page 190*

Saul and Jonathan were lovely and pleasant in their lives, and in their death they were not divided . . .
2 Samuel 1:23

Father, thank you for the gift of eternal bonds with my loved ones. It is comforting to know that, when I love someone, death does not part our love. I am thankful to know that my loved ones, there with you, can hear me, see me, and know that I love them still.

Affirmation: **The power of my love exists into the eternities, it never ends, it never dies.**

I Can Call Down the Powers of Heaven

Through prayer we bring life to our souls. Not only do we open ourselves to an increased endowment of God's love and light, but we also call down the powers of heaven to overcome trials. In sending up a desperate cry for help, we call angels down to our sides to fight for our cause by adding their energy to ours. *The Ripple Effect - page 95*

Lift up your eyes on high, and behold who hath created these things, that bringeth out their host by numbers: he calleth them all by names by the greatness of his might, for that he is strong in power; not one faileth. Isaiah 40:26

Father, how precious is your wisdom, how glorious your ways! Thank you for creating the perfect way to aid me when I cry out to you for help. Bless me to open the door to your powers by seeking you first in my trials.

Affirmation: **I ask, and mighty angels come to my aid and lend their strength to mine.**

The Veil of Forgetting
Protects Us

I now understood why it was important for us to go through the "veil of forgetting" when we come to earth . . . because remembering is so horrifically painful.
The Awakening Heart - pages 23-24

He has made every thing beautiful in his time: also he hath set the world in their heart, so that no man can find out the work that God maketh from the beginning to the end. *Ecclesiastes 3:11*

Father, how wise you are! Remembering my Heavenly Home would bring pain and distress of not being there. Often I wish I could remember my time with you. But in your wisdom, those memories were not mine to keep. Bless me, then, with an inner knowing of our unending bonds of love, so that I may live with greater hope and walk in greater faith.

Affirmation: **I walk by faith, each day more confident and sure of my beautiful home in heaven.**

God Blesses Me to Become
Pure in Heart

I was . . . led to Matthew 6:33: "But seek ye first the kingdom of God and his righteousness and all these things shall be added unto you." I had also been shown that the kingdom of God was within us, that we are the temple of God and he dwells there when we let him.
The Awakening Heart - page 30

*K*now ye not that ye are the temple of God, and that the Spirit of God dwelleth in you? *1 Corinthians 3:16*

*F*ather, bless me to become pure in heart and to find joy with you into the eternities. Anoint my soul to be a worthy temple, and to receive your Holy Spirit so that you will dwell within me forever.

Affirmation: **With rejoicing I invite God's anointing. His Spirit resides within me forever.**

I Am a Joint Heir with Jesus Christ

I knew [Jesus], his spirit, his feelings, his concern for me. I felt his kinship with me, and I knew that we were family. I felt that his relationship to me was both like a father and as older brother. He was close to me, but there was also an element of authority. He was tender and good natured, but also responsible. I knew with a sure knowledge that he would never misuse his authority, that he would never even desire to do so. *Embraced By The Light - page 73*

The Spirit itself beareth witness with our spirit, that we are the children of God: And if children, then heirs; heirs of God, and joint-heirs with Christ; if so be that we suffer with him, that we may be also glorified together. *Romans 8:16-17*

Thank you, Father, my spirit feels the unity and love of my Eternal Family. Bless me to remember that, like Jesus, I am responsible in sharing your eternal love. Help me never to fail to walk arm and arm with others to encourage and to bless.

Affirmation: **As a child of God, I am an heir with Christ and just as responsible.**

May 5

My Nature Is Expressed in My Body and Spirit

To dwell upon a thought is to give it energy. To act upon a thought is to give it life . . . When we give something place within our nature, it manifests itself physically and spiritually. Giving place to negative thoughts by repeating them, pondering them, gnawing on them, gives them energy and thus the power to transform us into their image. *The Ripple Effect - page 85*

Keep thy heart with all diligence; for out of it are the issues of life. *Proverbs 4:23*

Father, when a negative thought floods my mind, bless me to let its energy pass through without focusing on it, feeding it, and giving it greater energy to control my life. Thank you for teaching me how to direct my thoughts in creating loving realities which increase my inner peace and joy.

Affirmation: **My spirit is free to express in any way its true divine nature.**

My Spirit Yearns for Heavenly Joy

God created our spirits long before we were born on earth. I saw this clearly and repeatedly during my experience. In fact much of what I "learned" about heaven was actually a remembering of it from when I lived there before. I remembered it because, when we die, the veil of forgetfulness is removed from our minds. *The Ripple Effect - page 2*

Is there any thing whereof it may be said, See, this is new? it hath been already of old time, which was before us. Ecclesiastes 1:10

Father, when my spirit connects with distant memories of heaven, I feel homesick and lonely. Without understanding why, I often long for someone or some place that my mind can not recall. Even while family and friends surround me, I often feel incomplete. Please fill my aching heart with the comfort of your love and with the knowledge that you and those I miss in heaven are more near to me than I know.

Affirmation: **My spirit is in tune with all that was, is, and will be. I am comforted in that truth.**

God Blesses and Uses
Many Faiths

Many faiths on earth do not include Christ but are loved and used by God nevertheless. Our Father never turns away a person who searches for him . . . A person born to a home that does not recognize God is not cursed, but rather blessed with the needed opportunities of growth uniquely available in that home. Any person searching for any degree of light, in any religion or system of belief, is graced by God with opportunities for greater light. *The Ripple Effect - page 110*

Again, the kingdom of heaven is like unto a net, that was cast into the sea, and gathered of every kind . . . Matthew 13:47

Thank you, Father. You are a good shepherd, and I notice your care through your love for all your children. Forgive me when my mortal ego lays claim to possess a truth or a salvation which is not mine to claim exclusively. Bless me to know that you are limitless in your ways.

Affirmation: **I acknowledge the unlimited powers of God to reach and to hold all his children.**

May 8

My Aura of Light Reveals My True Spirit

Prayers take form as an energy that if visible would be seen to add light to our presence or the aura around us. Our souls glow brighter in prayer as our spirits communicate with the Divine, because we are made more divine by the act of honest communication with Deity. *The Ripple Effect - page 95*

If thy whole body therefore be full of light, having no part dark, the whole shall be full of light, as when the bright shining of a candle doth give thee light. Luke 11:36

Thank you, Father, for teaching me through scripture that, should I dispute with my brother, to make it right before I come to you in prayer. Help me to use this principle whenever I have let something go amiss in my life; to do my best to set things right before asking forgiveness of you. In this way, Father, I know you can bless my countenance with your light.

Affirmation: **Enlightenment comes to me in communication with the Father, and his glory fills my heart.**

May 9

I Am a
Child of God

*A*s God's spiritual children, we are a part of him. God is love, and love is in us, and that is our source of energy. It is natural for us to desire to love and to be loved. Sometimes we lose our ability to love, because it has been overshadowed by struggle, despair, anguish, and fears. But it is still there . . . to be recalled when we are ready. *The Awakening Heart - page 53*

Beloved, let us love one another: for love is of God; and every one that loveth is born of God, and knoweth God . . . for God is love. 1 John 4:7-8

Father, expand my god-like qualities of pure love to dispel all fear, anguish, and despair. Keep me in your likeness, and bless me to desire the full extent of it. Teach me all that I should do to live with you some day.

Affirmation: **I love, and in this, I express my creation and the will of my Creator .**

My Spirit Was Given Power Over My Flesh

*R*emembering that the spirit and the mind have tremendous influence on the flesh, I saw that we literally have power to affect our own health. I saw that the spirit in each of us is powerful, that it can give strength to the body to ward off illness, or, once the body is sick, to cause it to heal. The spirit has power to control the mind, and the mind controls the body. *Embraced By The Light - page 62*

*A*nd be renewed in the spirit of your mind . . . that ye put on the new man . . . *Ephesians, 4:23-24*

*F*ather, thank you for the tremendous power within me to heal my body and influence my health. Bless me to know how to use my spirit's abilities better so that, by combining this knowledge with my faith in you, I will enjoy health in mind and body.

Affirmation: **The power of spirit to renew myself daily keeps me healthy, strong and whole.**

The Creator Is
Acquainted with My Ways

*O*ur Creator understands the pains of this life. He lived it too. Through his omniscient knowledge, he makes perfect judgments. He knows who we are and exactly what we need at every moment of existence. *The Ripple Effect - page 207*

O *Lord, thou hast searched me, and known me . . . Thou compassest my path and my lying down, and art acquainted with all my ways. Psalms 139:1,3*

Father, how patient, gracious, and forgiving you are to love me even though I repeat my mistakes and am slow to learn. There is so much to overcome and to strengthen. Bless me to follow your will and to bear my burdens with greater capacity and nobility. I want with all my heart to be pleasing to you.

Affirmation: **My Creator knows all of my ways, and he guides and directs me to perfection.**

My Soul
Shines in Loveliness

To love others as myself, I first had to really love myself. The beauty and light of Christ were within me—he saw them!—and now I had to search within myself to find them as well . . . I saw that I had suppressed the genuine loveliness of my own soul. I had to let it shine again as it once had. *Embraced By The Light* - page 117

He that getteth wisdom loveth his own soul: he that keepeth understanding shall find good. Proverbs 19:8

Thank you, Father, for I am your creation, and the beauty of Christ's Spirit is part of my soul. Thank you for blessing me with your beauty and light so that I can learn to love these aspects of myself without condition. Bless me to grow more like you in truth and in love, that I might bear witness of your understanding and wisdom.

Affirmation: **I express the beauty and light of Christ, and God resides within my soul.**

May 13

My Suffering Can Be Used by God

As people choose a path not intended by God for them, they will eventually learn, but through a harder, longer process than necessary. Regardless of the process, though, whether in this life or in the next, it will yet turn them to God . . . Every knee shall bow and every tongue confess. God will use any means at his command to reclaim his lost children—even if it is through the things which they suffer. *The Ripple Effect - page 87*

For I reckon that the sufferings of this present time are not worthy to be compared with the glory which shall be revealed in us. Romans 8:18

Father, thank you for blessing me in suffering and for showing me that all things work out for those who love the Lord. Bless me in trial to see the situation more clearly, and how to find resolution. Help me turn all my difficulties into growth, that I may glorify you in all things.

Affirmation: **My life glorifies God, my creator, who turns my weaknesses and pain to my good.**

I Prepare My Spirit for the Abundance of God

*U*nder the guidance of the Savior I learned that it was important for me to accept all experience as potentially good. I needed to accept my purpose and station in life. I could take the negative things that had happened to me and try to overcome their effects . . . I saw that I could begin to heal myself, spiritually first, then emotionally, mentally and physically. I saw that I could spare myself the corrosive effects of despair, I had a right to live fully. *Embraced By The Light - page 69*

I am come that they might have life, and that they might have it more abundantly. John 10:10

Father, how grateful I am to experience mortal life. Through its times of joys and sorrows I am refined and learn to live in accordance with your great plan of happiness for me. Open me to your great abundance, Father, and ease my limiting attitudes. For nothing which can bless me is scarce in you or in your creation.

Affirmation: **I honor God by embracing my life and preparing my spirit in expectation of abundance.**

May 15

Only the Creator Knows
My Purpose

We need to be careful in judging whether or not someone has fulfilled his mission. A person who appears to be failing may in fact be learning more quickly than a person who appears successful. Our Creator knows which weaknesses we come with and which experiences we require for spiritual growth.
The Ripple Effect - page 22

He hath shewed thee, O man, what is good; and what doth the Lord require of thee, but to do justly, and to love mercy, and to walk humbly with thy God?
Micah 6:8

Father, when I see imperfections in others, help me refrain from condemning them, supposing them to be misguided. Teach me to walk in humility and kindness, and to remember that you guide all your children in the uniqueness of their missions. Bless me to focus less on faults and failures and more on strengths and successes. Help me encourage others on their paths and become stronger myself in these attributes.

Affirmation: **I withhold judgement and pray for understanding instead.**

May 16

My Countenance Expresses the Spirit of Love

I had also witnessed that God is love, and I knew that without love in my heart—not just for others, but for myself—I was lost. I no longer loved my mortal self; I had seen my spiritual being. This body was like clay, heavy, cumbersome, and abhorrent to me.
The Awakening Heart - page 31

It is the spirit that quickeneth; the flesh profiteth nothing . . . *John 6:63*

Father, while I live in my mortal body, help me to love it and find peace with it. Help me recognize and make use of the love you have instilled in my spirit so I can glorify my flesh. Let me live in the knowledge of that divine portion of my being which is more truly me, and not indulge in the weakness of my flesh. Bless me to bring each part into harmony. And guide me toward the ability to use my eternal nature and the power of both my spirit and body to rise above the things of this world.

Affirmation: **My body and its countenance express the eternal beauty of my spirit.**

May 17

Good Works Bring Me Hope and Peace

The road back from darkness is seldom easy or quick. Daily effort is required to stay on course, but a whole new world awaits at the end, if we persist. As we pray for help and stop thinking so much of our own misery, seeking instead to serve others, we will find peace in our souls. This service, combined with self-forgiveness and faith that God has already forgiven us, will renew us in spirit and grant us more energy to pursue the opportunities before us. *The Ripple Effect - page 208*

Now our Lord Jesus Christ himself, and God, even our Father, which hath loved us, and hath given us everlasting consolation and good hope through grace, Comfort your hearts, and establish you in every good word and work. 2 Thessalonians 2:16-17

Father, as I travel through this darkened world, bless me with opportunities to serve you. For when I am in service, I am able to see you in others, and I find light and peace for myself.

Affirmation: **I am renewed in Spirit and find peace, hope and light in every work I do.**

 May 18

My Creator Knew Me
Before This Earth

I knew that God hears *all* prayers and answers them in their right time, according to his plan for each of us. *The Awakening Heart - page 24*

*B*lessed be the God and Father of our Lord Jesus Christ, who hath blessed us with all spiritual blessings in heavenly places in Christ: According as he hath chosen us in him before the foundation of the world . . . *Ephesians 1:3-4*

*F*ather, when you knitted me in the womb of my mother, you knew me, even to the number of hairs on my head. You knew my future and all of its possibilities, even giving me use of free will to chose my way. Your plan for me in place now, you watch over me from where you are, waiting as an anxious parent to hear from me in prayer, ready to help and to bless. Thank you, Father, for your constancy and your loving guidance as I walk the path prepared for me.

Affirmation: **My Heavenly Father knows my heart, hears my prayers, and answers them according to his plans for me.**

Jesus Radiates God's Eternal Love

I was told that all truth eventually leads to Christ—even if we have to find him in the next life. Each person returning to the spirit world will come to know that Jesus Christ is the Son of God and that he was sent by our Father to restore His truth.

The Ripple Effect - page 109

And we have seen and do testify that the Father sent the Son to be the Saviour of the world. 1 John 4:14

Father, thank you for sending Jesus to restore the truth of your unconditional love. He shows me by his own life how best to live, and that the way back home to you is simple, defined, and uncomplicated by the doctrines of mankind. Thank you, Jesus, for the gate through which I will return to the Father . . . is called love.

Affirmation: **I travel the simple, well marked path of love on my journey home to my creator.**

God's Comforting Peace
Removes All Fear

$\mathcal{D}$arkness began to surround my entire being . . . And immediately I was gently drawn up and into a great, whirling, black mass . . . But there was no fear. I felt a process of healing take place. Love filled this whirling, moving mass, and I sank more deeply into its warmth and blackness and rejoiced in my security and peace. I thought, "This must be where the valley of the shadow of death is." I had never felt greater tranquility in my life.
Embraced By The Light - pages 37-39

$\mathcal{Y}$ea, though I walk through the valley of the shadow of death, I will fear no evil: for thou art with me; thy rod and thy staff they comfort me. Psalms 23:4

$\mathcal{T}$hank you, Father, for your comforting arms that always surround me. When my time draws near to return to you, your loving presence will guide me through the unfamiliar passage. Bless me to hold onto your Spirit for safety and peace until I leave my earthly body to run to you.

Affirmation: **When it is my time to leave, I will transform like a butterfly to be greeted by God and my loved ones.**

May 21

God's Voice Is
Clear and Distinct

One night God made it clear to me that our relationship was a two-way street. I was sleeping soundly when I heard a loud voice . . . "Get up and pray." . . . I hurried out of bed and knelt beside it . . . I asked Heavenly Father to reveal to me who I should pray for . . . The answer came back that he just wanted to hear from me and that the prayer was more for my own benefit than anyone else's . . . *The Awakening Heart - page 46*

They should seek the Lord . . . and find him, though he be not far from every one of us: For in him we live, and move, and have our being . . . For we are also his offspring. Acts 17:27-28

Father, forgive me when I am tired and my mind is too dim to stay awake during my prayers. Sometimes I am weary and worn out from my same old problems, and I hesitate to keep bringing them to you. Help me to keep in mind that you already know my heart and what I will pray for, but still are wanting to listen to me.

Affirmation: **God is anxious to converse with me, and answers back in a sweet and clear voice.**

Only God's Judgement
Is Perfect

God weighs not only the actions of a person but the intents of the heart as well. Because [he judges with] perfect knowledge and love, we could never receive a more thorough or merciful judgment by any other means.
The Ripple Effect - page 88

Then hear thou in heaven thy dwelling place, and forgive, and do, and give to every man according to his ways, whose heart thou knowest; (for thou, even thou only, knowest the hearts of all the children of men;) 1 Kings 8:39

Thank you for teaching me, Father. As a parent, I am learning how to discern the hearts of my children. I know the strengths and weaknesses of each child. I see how they differ not only in intent, but also how they carry out their intentions. There is not one of my children I could stop loving . . . no matter what they did . . . nor is there one that I would not lay down my life for. You are perfect in these ways, Father, and I am confident that you forgive me in your infinite understanding and patience.

Affirmation: **My Father in heaven knows my heart and judges all that is best within me.**

May 23

Before I Cry Out to God, He Hears Me

The time spent in prayer during the first and last few minutes of the day can keep your spirit in tune with God. Prayers do not need to be elaborate; my own are often quite simple, like conversation with a parent or a heartfelt "good morning" or "good night" expressed with appreciation for God's love and generosity. Since taking the time to create the habit of prayer, I have felt closer to God in my thoughts, words, and deeds.

The Awakening Heart - pages 221-222

And it shall come to pass, that before they call, I will answer: and while they are yet speaking , I will hear. Isaiah 65:24

Father, my love for you grows stronger each time I think of how you bless my life. And you bless me to know that I am important to you no matter what is happening in my life— and that your Spirit hovers near me—and hears my heart before I have time to express it in my thoughts, feelings, or words. Thank you for your nurturing and mentoring love.

Affirmation: **My heart is in tune with God; he hears me before I pray.**

Positive Thoughts Create Positive Lives

There is power in our thoughts. We create our own surroundings by the thoughts we think. Physically, this may take a period of time, but spiritually it is instantaneous. If we understood the power of our thoughts, we would guard them more closely . . . All creation begins in the mind . . . Thoughts are deeds. *Embraced By The Light - pages 58-59*

Whatsoever things are true, whatsoever things are honest, whatsoever things are just, whatsoever things are pure, whatsoever things are lovely, whatsoever things are of good report; if there be any virtue, and if there be any praise, think on these things. Philippians 4:8

Thank you, Father, for guiding me in how to govern my thoughts. Your instructions are perfect and praiseworthy. Help me to use the power of my mind to bless all that surrounds me. Keep my thoughts pure, honest and kind.

Affirmation: **Since all that I create begins in my mind, I think on virtuous things.**

In Choosing Good, I Change Generations to Come

We have the God-given right and the ability to create waves of positive emotion rather than of terror and abuse. We can send our children on to their own children with backgrounds of love and kindness and patience, or we can deliver them over to the same hells we may have received from our own parents. We face the choice everyday. In every difficulty we can choose to create something new and healthy or to recycle the poison of generations past.
The Ripple Effect - page 48

Choose you this day whom ye will serve; whether the gods which your fathers served that were on the other side of the flood . . . but as for me and my house, we will serve the Lord. Joshua 24:15

Father, thank you for the gift of choice. Help me never use it to spread grief and misery, but to bless my family and friends with waves of warmth and love. Sustain me in my choice to treat others with a Christ-like spirit and to serve you in my home.

Affirmation: **I create a haven of peace and love which ripples out through my family and friends for generations to come.**

May 26

The Ripple Effect at Its Finest Is to Share God's Love

Share the power of God's love with others. This is the ripple effect at its finest, creating waves of positive energy that are full of love, going forward until one day that love will be experienced by all. *The Ripple Effect - page xi*

The love of God is shed abroad in our hearts . . .
Romans 5:5

Father, help me to live the example of Jesus in loving others unconditionally and completely. I desire with all my heart to emulate him, and to show charity and kindness to everyone and to carry good will in my heart always. Bless me to fulfill your will by all I do, and let the consequence of this ripple out into the heart of every man, woman and child I meet.

Affirmation: **Willingly and gratefully I share the love of God with all.**

Internalizing What I Learn Develops Faith

Now I understood that in my misery I had lost my faith in God. I remembered I had been told knowledge comes before faith, and while it was clear that I had knowledge of his existence, had even experienced his presence, I realized now that I had not internalized it, made it a part of me. *The Awakening Heart - page 31*

Behold, thou desirest truth in the inward parts: and in the hidden part thou shalt make me to know wisdom. Psalms 51:6

Father, how miserable life is without faith in you and in your eternal love. Help me to endure the tests of my faith and the trials they bring as I grow in understanding and knowledge of you. Help me pull what I learn of you deep into my being to become a sure foundation of hope and faith. No shift or change or turmoil can shake my certainty of you or your love, Father.

Affirmation: **My heart is faithful to God and hungers for his truth.**

May 28

My Prayers Benefit Both
Heaven and Earth

I was told that our prayers can benefit both spiritual beings as well as persons on the earth. If there is reason to fear for a departed person's spirit, if there is reason to believe their transition may be difficult or unwanted, we can pray for them and enlist spiritual help. *Embraced By The Light - page 84*

For God is my witness, whom I serve with my spirit in the gospel of his Son, that without ceasing I make mention of you always in my prayers . . . Romans 1:9

Father, your blessings of power in my thoughts and words are so great that when I speak them in prayer, they reach you in heaven. This gift is powerful in blessing my loved ones both here and there with you. Thank you for gifting me with creative energy and teaching me to use it in my prayers.

Affirmation: **My prayers for others reach into heaven and touch the lives of even the spirits there.**

I May Discern
Angels of Light

Angels may come to us in dreams since they are able to enter our thoughts when authorized by God to do so. We must not fear them, but receive their message with gratitude and humility. We can know if a message or an angel is from God because we will sense no darkness in them. No unclean thought or thing can come from God. We can test their spirits by remembering this. *The Ripple Effect - page 11*

And of the angels he saith, Who maketh his angels spirits, and his ministers a flame of fire. Hebrews 1:7

Father, my spirit is open to receiving your word only. Because of this, I know that no unclean thought or messenger comes from you. Thank you for your protection and for giving me a way to discern spirits of truth.

Affirmation: **I am open to messengers of God and know them by the love and truth within them.**

Children Convey Innocence and Love from God

Our tender children are precious to God. They come to us straight from him—innocent, trusting, and forgiving. They bring the light and love of God with them and willingly place their untouched hearts into our hands to be molded as we choose. *The Ripple Effect - page 48*

But Jesus said, Suffer little children, and forbid them not, to come unto me; for of such is the kingdom of heaven. *Matthew 19:14*

Thank you, Father, for gifting the world with children who teach us your ways and bring us joy. When I see a new baby, I think of how it represents your love and presence. I think of its innocence and of our responsibility to keep its heart untouched by pain. Bless the world to know that these precious angels are not ours to abuse, but to love and to keep safe for you. Bless the childlike part of me to remain tender and moldable in your loving hands.

Affirmation: **I am God's spirit child, and he conditions my heart to keep me innocent, trusting and forgiving.**

The Spirit of a Prayer
Affects Its Energy

It is our desires, not the wording or form we use, that provides the energy that makes our prayers effective. Without a desire to connect with God, our prayers become hollow and meaningless. But with true desire, our prayers not only ascend to heaven, but they nurture as well. *The Ripple Effect - page 95*

I will pray with the spirit, and I will pray with the understanding also: I will sing with the spirit, and I will sing with the understanding also. 1 Corinthians 14:15

Father, bless me to pray with true desire in my heart. Help me to feel what I am praying for and to imagine it being done. Thank you for hearing me when I cry out to you in moments of deep emotion. I know you understand even the feelings which I cannot express in words. Let me never fall into the habit of routine, half-felt prayers, but rather always come to you with real intent, with a heart full of purpose and faith.

Affirmation: **My desire connects me with God to be nurtured at his side.**

June 1

God Forgives My Sins and Forgets Them

I understood that forgiven sins are blotted out. It is as if they are overlaid by new understanding, by a new direction in life. This new understanding then leads me to naturally abandon the sin. Although the sin is blotted out, however, the educational part of the experience remains. Thus the forgiven sin helps me to grow and increases my ability to help others. *Embraced By The Light - pages 115-116*

*B*lessed is he whose transgression is forgiven, whose sin is covered. *Psalms 32:1*

*F*ather, thank you for your forgiveness when I do things on my own without you and fail. Bless me to use my experiences to overcome weakness and to gain understanding of the wrong I have done. Help me to make things right again and in all things to turn to you first so that I may become a greater blessing and help to others.

Affirmation: **God forgives my sins and mistakes, and I have grown in greater wisdom of Him and myself.**

My Soul Is of Infinite Worth

No one is insignificant in the eternities. Every soul is of infinite worth. *Embraced By The Light - page 121*

What man of you, having an hundred sheep, if he lose one of them, doth not leave the ninety and nine in the wilderness, and go after that which is lost, until he find it? *Luke 15:4*

Father, my worth is measured by your love for me which is unconditional, everlasting, eternal and completely mine. Thank you for empowering me with your love and for seeing me as one who completes the whole. I know that it is your will to reclaim every one of your children, and I thank you for never letting me stray far from you. You truly are a perfect Creator.

Affirmation: **I am significant and of infinite worth to God, my Creator.**

I Move Beyond My Past to Find God

Life is like a river . . . Some people believe that the circumstances of youth set an unchangeable course for their river. But, life is dynamic, and the river stretches and bends as we go. A bad beginning does not inevitably lead to a bad ending. In fact a bad beginning can give us strength to create a good ending. *The Ripple Effect - pages 28-29*

The night is far spent, the day is at hand: let us therefore cast off the works of darkness, and let us put on the armor of light. Romans 13:12

Father, I do not want past perceptions and understandings to cast shadows on my future. Bless me to let go of those events and circumstances which I no longer have control over. Help me instead to create a greater future for myself and for those I love. Thank you, Father, for opening my eyes to possibilities for change.

Affirmation: **I am free from my past and open to new experiences blessed by God's love.**

My Spirit Seeks
Harmony with My Flesh

Spiritually, we are at various degrees of light—which is knowledge—and because of our divine, spiritual nature we are filled with the desire to do good. Our earthly selves, however, are constantly in opposition to our spirits . . . Although our spirit bodies are full of light, truth, and love, they must battle constantly to overcome the flesh, and this strengthens them. Those who are truly developed will find a perfect harmony between their flesh and spirits, a harmony that will bless them with peace and give them the ability to help others.
Embraced By The Light - page 50

That the man of God may be perfect, throughly furnished unto all good works. 2 Timothy 3:17

Father, I am grateful for the knowledge you have placed within me and for the flesh that temporarily houses my soul. Bless me to achieve balance in soul and body and in all things, that I might create perfect harmony in my life and in the world, as well.

Affirmation: **I am God's perfect creation and enjoy harmony and balance within my soul.**

I Am
Learning to Love

Our distortions and misunderstanding of love can often lead to pain. God allows this pain because he wants us to learn what real love is and what it is not. He wants us to learn that true love, pure love, is giving and sharing without ego. That it is constant, eternal, and unconditional. *The Ripple Effect - page 151*

Let love be without dissimulation . . . Be kindly affectioned one to another with brotherly love; in honour preferring one another. Romans 12:9-10

Father, like everyone in life, I have made some mistakes while learning how to love. Thank you for seeing me through those times and for helping me see the false direction and attachments that brought pain and disappointment to me and to those I sought love from. Bless me with a more perfect understanding of love, so that as I love again, I will give and receive the kind of love which makes everything whole.

Affirmation: **I love without expectation or condition, which fills my heart with joy.**

Mortality Is for Me to Learn to Serve

Whatever we become here in mortality is meaningless unless it is done for the benefit of others. Our gifts and talents are given to us to help us serve. And in serving others we grow spiritually. *Embraced By The Light - page 50*

That ye present your bodies a living sacrifice, holy, acceptable unto God, which is our reasonable service. Romans 12:1

Father, I want to lose my life in the service of others. Bless me to be aware of daily opportunities to serve, and strengthen me to serve wherever I am needed. Help me discover the gifts and abilities you have placed within me to bless others, Father. And expand my heart in using them with generosity and love towards all. Thank you for the joyous feelings that come as I serve and which make me feel closer to you.

Affirmation: **I live my life most completely because my efforts help make the world a happier and better place.**

Even Simple Truth
Blesses Me

As people explore truths at one level, a desire awakens in them for the next level. And that level—whatever it may be—is the next step in that person's individual growth. I understood that everything which awakens us to truth is good. And that even the simplest of truths are better than no truth at all.
The Ripple Effect - page 109

And ye shall know the truth, and the truth shall make you free. John 8:32

Thank you, Father, for instilling the desire for truth in me. And thank you for sending teachers and others to give me truths and to strengthen my desire to learn even more. Bless me to be open to acquiring knowledge of you. I know you will only give what is right for my spirit.

Affirmation: **My spirit rejoices in truth and the freedom that it brings.**

I Live in a
Chosen Generation

This crazy mind-boggling world is ours. We chose to come to it, and we chose this period of time in which to come. Many of us were among the strong ones, ready and determined to come and bless this world in these chaotic times. Now's our chance. *The Ripple Effect - page 91*

Ye are a chosen generation . . . a peculiar people; that ye should show forth the praises of him who hath called you out of darkness into his marvelous light. 1 Peter 2:9

Father, my life may seem meaningless and hectic at times, but I know that through your wisdom you placed me in the right place at the right time. Thank you for the opportunity to bear witness of you through the expression of my life, and bless me with the strength and determination to see my mission through.

Affirmation: **My life is a joy to my Creator and me. Together we will see it through.**

God Guides Me to Meekness and Humility

*M*atthew 7:7: "Ask, and it shall be given you . . ." Ask? I had done that, but I hadn't been focused enough to know what to ask for. And though I had asked for help, I had not been open to receive it until I let go of my ego and allowed God to guide me to the answers, as he did now. *The Awakening Heart - page 31*

The meek will he guide in judgment: and the meek will he teach his way. Psalms 25:9

Father, thank you for your direction. Simplicity is the best route to finding answers, so bless me when my ego wants to complicate things and I get caught up in my own wisdom. Teach me to become more humble, more meek, that I remain teachable and open to receive honest and direct answers from you.

Affirmation: **My spirit humbly recognizes the powerful Spirit of God and listens for his guidance.**

A Single Act Can
Last Forever

$\mathcal{E}$verything we do ripples out; we affect others, and they in turn affect us. Sometimes the ripples create huge waves that wash over humanity, changing it forever, as Christ's life did. Sometimes they are so small that they remain relatively unknown in this lifetime. *The Ripple Effect - page xi*

Then shall thy light break forth as the morning . . . and thy righteousness shall go before thee; the glory of the Lord shall be thy reward. Isaiah 58:8

Father, bless me to become more aware of my single acts and to see them as seeds to a greater harvest. Though my entire life may consist of only smaller ripples, I desire them to glorify you. Thank you for blessing me to know that I must be mindful of all that I say and do.

Affirmation: **My every action is filled with love and blesses more than I know.**

In Listening to My Heart, I Rediscover Truth

The knowledge of what has always been remains in us, as part of his plan for us. Sometimes we call it intuition, at other times . . . inspiration. When we follow our hearts, when we are in tune and balanced, and when we listen to the still inner voice within us . . . we "know." *The Awakening Heart - page 53*

I communed with mine own heart . . . yea, my heart had great experience of wisdom and knowledge. Ecclesiastes 1:16

What joy there is, Father, in awakening to the resources of my heart. The inspirations it gives when I am in tune with you bless my life and never fail me. Bless me to look within first, and then to follow my heart.

Affirmation: **My heart is a reservoir of knowledge, and I go there often to drink from its wisdom.**

My Spirit Understands Universal Language

The spirit speaks a universal language, deeper and more powerful than voice. It communicates accurately and clearly, piercing through mankind's ignorance or false understandings and recognizing each person's true desires. *The Ripple Effect - page 95*

But God hath revealed them unto us by his Spirit: for the spirit searcheth all things, yea, the deep things of God. *1 Corinthians 2:10*

Father, thank you for teaching me that, when I quiet my mind and listen with my heart, I will hear more accurately and understand more clearly. Help me to be still and to hear your spirit's voice.

Affirmation: **My spirit speaks through my heart and reveals to me my true desire .**

I Can Learn to Create Abundance

We are sent here to live life fully, to live it abundantly, to find joy in our own creations, whether they are new thoughts or things or emotions or experiences. We are to create our own lives, to exercise our gifts and experience both failure and success. We are to use our free will to expand and magnify our lives. *Embraced By The Light - page 59*

Give her of the fruit of her hands; and let her own works praise her in the gates. *Proverbs 31:31*

Father, thank you for the opportunity to test my ability to be fruitful. There is great joy in using my talents in accomplishment, and power in knowing I have personal strengths. Open my eyes to new ways of using what I have to create what I need and desire. And may I always share my abundance with others in a loving way, thus keeping myself open to your blessings and increasing my ability to receive more.

Affirmation: **I magnify my life and glorify God with my fruitfulness.**

I Am Timeless

I had a difficult time comprehending the concept of eternity, let alone eternities. Eternity to me had always been in the future, but these beings said they had been with me for eternities in the past. This was more difficult to comprehend. Then I began to see images in my mind of a time long ago, of an existence before my life on earth, of my relationship with these men "before."

Embraced By The Light - page 31

When there were no depths, I was brought forth . . . Before the mountains were settled, before the hills was I brought forth: While as yet he had not made the earth, nor the fields, nor the highest part of the dust of the world. When he prepared the heavens, I was there . . .

Proverbs 8:24-27

When this life is through, I pray, Father, that my spirit will once again rejoice in remembrance of the many loved ones who await my return. Strengthen my awareness that I am a timeless being, that my life on earth is a continuation of my eternal existence.

Affirmation: **I will one day return to my eternal home, and I rejoice.**

My Work of Faith Is a Labor of Love

*E*ach person's life is multifaceted, and we should trust the power of God and his angels to give us every opportunity we need to succeed. Our part is to seek to improve ourselves and, above all, to love others more fully. By praying for guidance and letting love rule our hearts and minds each day, we will eventually accomplish our many purposes. *The Ripple Effect - page 21*

*R*emembering without ceasing your work of faith, and labour of love, and patience of hope in our Lord Jesus Christ . . . *1 Thessalonians 1:3*

*F*ather, I seek your guidance in fulfilling the promises I made to you before coming to this earth. Lead me to accomplish them, even though I might not recall the nature of them. And bless me with the purest of motivation and love as I do my work. Always keep me faithful to the love and hope of Jesus Christ.

Affirmation: **My missions are accomplished through the love of Jesus Christ and by my faith in him.**

I Am Reborn
Through Death

The fact of a pre-earth life crystallized in my mind, and I saw that death was actually a "rebirth" into a greater life of understanding and knowledge that stretched forward and backward through time. *Embraced By The Light - pages 31-32*

In hope of eternal life, which God, that cannot lie, promised before the world began . . . Titus 1:2

Thank you, Father, your promise of a greater life after this one blesses me in many ways. It helps me to feel less afraid to die and gives me a measure of peace when I hear of the many, seemingly senseless deaths that occur here on earth. Thank you for your promise that we live again, that life for everyone is eternal.

Affirmation: **My time on earth is but a tiny sliver of my existence which stretches forward and backward through eternity.**

Angels Hover
Over Me

During my experience I saw many angels hovering over people on earth, attempting to communicate with them or to guide them. Most of the people, however, refused to hear them. If you are open to the gifts and words of God, you will receive the answers and directions you need in life.
The Ripple Effect - page 11

And the angel of the Lord called unto him out of heaven, and said, Abraham, Abraham: and he said, Here am I. Genesis 22:11

Father, thank you for sending angels when I need them, whether I am aware of their presence or not. Bless me to hear the sweetness of their voices and to know that they are messengers sent by you.

Affirmation: **I listen for the voices of angels and am open to receive their messages from God.**

With Growth I Turn
Negative to Positive

We may see people facing one challenge on top of another and wonder whether they can take one more thing. Their growth is enhanced by their willingness to take what appear to be negative events and turn them into something very positive. These individuals continue to grow and expand at a tremendous rate, unlike others whose lives just drift along.

The Awakening Heart - page 218

Be of good courage, and he shall strengthen your heart, all ye that hope in the Lord. Psalms 31:24

Father, thank you for blessing my life with courage to experience all that I was sent here to explore. I willingly accept every challenge that will expand my awareness and bless my life to serve others. Bless me as I grow, and strengthen me when I am weak. In every trial that would bring me down, help me find the energy that will make me rise again.

Affirmation: **I accept challenge and face disappointments in eagerness to serve my Heavenly Father.**

I Know God to Be
My Heavenly Father

I began to think of God as more of a father in my [prayers] with him . . . We talked together as parent and child. I shared with him my joys and fears. I began to thank him for the things in which he expressed himself, which was just about everything.
The Awakening Heart - page 46

But to us there is but one God, the Father, of whom are all things, and we in him . . . 1 Corinthians 8:6

Father, oh, how sweet is your name. Your love and desire for me to accept you overwhelms my soul and brings tears to my heart. Thank you for our precious relationship, and for the love and strength your presence brings to me. Bless me each day to draw closer to you, to communicate with you daily, and to desire more than anything else to become one with you.

Affirmation: **My Father in heaven shares my joys and fears with the love and patience of a kind parent.**

To Love Is Life's Supreme Lesson

*A*bove all, I was shown that love is supreme. I saw that truly without love we are nothing. We are here to help each other, to care for each other, to understand, forgive, and serve one another. We are here to have love for every person born on earth. *Embraced By The Light - page 51*

A new commandment I give unto you, That ye love one another; as I have loved you, that ye also love one another. By this shall all men know that ye are my disciples, if ye have love one to another. John 13:34-35

Father, help me to think of others before myself, to understand and to accept differences without condemnation. Create in me Christ's love, that I may stand before you without blemish.

Affirmation: **The love that I share is supreme and blesses the world that I live in.**

I Am Worthy of God's Love and Protection

We are God's children and are worthy of love. No matter what has been done in the past or who we are today, we are worthy not only of God's unconditional love, but of self-love as well. Criticism may have shrunk our spirits, abuse may have damaged us, violence may have wounded us, but we are worthy of love. *The Ripple Effect - page 155*

He delivers me from my strong enemy, and from them that hated me . . . He brought me forth also into a large place: he delivered me, because he delighted in me. 2 Samuel 22:18, 20

Thank you, Father, for protecting me and delivering me from my enemies. From those who would harm me, and from those things I allow in my life that do harm. My heart has yearned for deliverance, but I have not always felt worthy of your love. Bless me to feel your delight in me, to trust that nothing is strong enough to stand against me nor remove your love from me ever.

Affirmation: **The being that I am, is worthy of God's unconditional love and protection.**

June 22

There Are No Coincidences in Life

*B*ecause our spirits remember the plan we chose for this life, we are often drawn to people or situations that impact us in important ways. This is often the force behind "chance" encounters. I was told there are no coincidences. However, making the most of these opportunities is up to us as we exercise our free will. *The Ripple Effect - page 20*

*L*ord, thou . . . hast wrought all our works in us. *Isaiah 26:12*

*F*ather, you have blessed me with numerous opportunities and with people to share them with me. Thank you for supplying all my needs. Bless me as I work my way through life to accept all that comes, not as chance or luck, but as placed there by your hand for my growth.

Affirmation: **I am open for greater opportunities to express myself and to help my spirit grow.**

I Progress at My Own Pace

Spiritual progression is not a race. We proceed at our own pace. But we should never put it off. By opening ourselves to new truths and greater faith, we increase in light. *The Ripple Effect - page 110*

O send out thy light and thy truth: let them lead me; let them bring me unto thy holy hill . . . Psalms 43:3

Thank you, Father, your light and truth bless my path and lead me to those things blessed by your love. As I grow in faith and in spirit, help me to remember that those around me have their own timing and position and purpose in life. Bless me to help them when needed but not push them along, and keep me from expecting more than what they can give. Continue blessing me with light as I am able to receive, and keep me from comparing my level of growth against that of others.

Affirmation: **I accept my role and the roles of others as perfect in God's eyes.**

Love Governs My Spirit

*L*ove always governs the spirit, and the spirit must be strengthened to rule the mind and flesh. I understood the natural order of love everywhere. First, we must love the Creator. This is the greatest love we can have. Then we must love ourselves. I knew that without feelings of self-love that the love we feel for others is counterfeit. Then, we must love all others as ourselves. As we see the light of Christ in ourselves, we will see it in others too, and it will become impossible not to love that part of God in them.
Embraced By The Light - pages 59-60

*F*or all the law is fulfilled in one word, even in this; Thou shalt love thy neighbour as thyself.
Galatians 5:14

*I*t is not always easy, Father, to truly love myself. Sometimes I feel unworthy even of your love for me. Help me to grow closer to you and to feel your divine spirit within me so that I can love myself and express that same love to my neighbors.

Affirmation: **My love for God extends to myself and to others.**

God Sees Past My Perception to Know My Heart

Everything we express in our energy fields comes from our perception, the filter through which we understand the world . . . God goes beyond the field and "knows" our hearts, our intent. *The Awakening Heart - page 51*

For the Lord searcheth all hearts, and understandeth all the imaginations of the thoughts . . . *1 Chronicles 28:9*

Father, thank you for the gift to create my world with my own thoughts and understandings. Help me to think of all things as blessings and to look upon them as a child might with interest and wonderment. Let me not miss one golden moment of experiencing the beauty of your creation. And when I see things amiss and make poor choices, it comforts me to know that you see within my heart my desires for good.

Affirmation: **This is the day that the Lord has created for me to rejoice and be glad in.**

Faith Is Action

*A*sk. Seek. Knock. These are action words of faith. But before any of these could be applied, I had to have desire as my driving force. I had that now, and I knew that my continued journey would require a powerful faith, in God, in me, and in the world that surrounds me. *The Awakening Heart - page 31*

*A*sk, and it shall be given you; seek, and ye shall find; knock, and it shall be opened unto you . . . *Matthew 7:7*

*F*ather, the gifts that await me are mine when I have faith to receive them. Thank you for trusting me with their stewardship, and for blessing me to use them in faith to magnify your glory.

Affirmation: **I act in faith to search all avenues in my life and to use my God-given talents.**

The Strength of Warring Angels Is Their Love

Warring Angels protect us from evil forces, from destructive thoughts, and from the unfair tactics of Satan. They see to it that our course is clear to do God's will. However, we are always to exercise our own faith. God will bless us with a clear path to do his work only after a trial of our faith and after we have prayed for protection and guidance.
The Ripple Effect - page 12

Thither cause thy mighty ones to come down, O Lord.
Joel 3:11

Father, how great is the force of the mighty angels who are given charge to watch over us! Thank you for sending them to protect me, as I accept your will in my life, and to shield me from destructive energies by the strength of their love.

Affirmation: **Warring angels stand by to protect me with the strength of their mighty love.**

Spiritual Experiences
Are to Be Shared

Spiritual experiences need to be shared. In my experience, Jesus told me that we are not to hide the truth; we are to share it with one another, to speak of the wonders and mysteries of God as they have been gifted to us. *The Ripple Effect - page xii*

The God of our fathers hath chosen thee, that thou shouldest know his will, and see that Just One, and shouldest hear the voice of his mouth. For thou shalt be his witness unto all men of what thou hast seen and heard. Acts 22:14-15

Father, forgive me the times I have not spoken up to share my wonderful witness with you, fearing that others would condemn me for believing and having faith in you. I know now to shout from the rooftops and to release joy from my soul. I promise my love to you and I will bear witness to the greatness of your glorious Spirit.

Affirmation: **I freely and joyfully witness to others of our Heavenly Father and his love.**

My Creator's Abilities
Are Limitless

I remembered that God was the creator of many worlds, galaxies, and realms beyond our understanding, and I wanted to see them . . . Two different beings of light . . . became my guides. Our spiritual bodies floated away . . . and into the blackness of space. I felt the exhilaration of flight . . . I entered the vastness of space and learned that it is not a void; it was full of love and light—the tangible presence of the Spirit of God. *Embraced By The Light - pages 86-87*

God . . . *hath in these last days spoken unto us by his Son, whom he hath appointed heir of all things, by whom also he made the worlds* . . . *Hebrews 1:2*

Father, the vastness of your glory and creation is incomprehensible to me. Yet I feel within it and within me your tangible presence. Thank you for sharing your creation and for blessing us with this world in which to live and to grow.

Affirmation: **My universe, like God, evolves and progresses endlessly.**

June 30

God Heightens
Spiritual Awareness

$\mathcal{S}$pirit continued to manifest itself in me…
My heightened state of spiritual awareness
made me more intense. I became more
keenly aware in all my senses, even my taste,
touch and smell. *The Awakening Heart - page 48*

*All the body by joints ministered, and knit together,
increaseth with the increase of God. Colossians 2:19*

*Father, to share in your presence is to grow
in greatness and in love. Thank you for
your countenance of beauty and your eagerness
to grace me with it. Awaken all my senses to
your love, and bless me to share that love with
others and to bask in it in remembrance of you.*

Affirmation: **My flesh bears witness of the
love of God, and expands in spiritual awareness by his Spirit.**

My Afflictions Serve Life's Purpose

Natural afflictions of the world come for many reasons, but we must put them all under the general heading of "Blessings." Some afflictions come as a result of personal choice . . . Some physical conditions occur as a result of our spiritual health. But every opposition is a gift from God and can be used to refine spiritual awareness and increase love if we choose to use them that way.
The Ripple Effect - page 90

Therefore I take pleasure in infirmities, in reproaches, in necessities, in persecutions, in distresses for Christ's sake: for when I am weak, then am I strong.
2 Corinthians 12:10

Father, natural disasters present great challenges in the world. Keep your Spirit near me when these occur. Calm my fears and strengthen me to survive afflictions. Bless me with insight to understand your purposes, and perfect my spirit that I might live through all that is required of me in a pure Christ-like way.

Affirmation: **My weaknesses point to great strengths and blessings which refine my soul.**

July 2

My Imperfect Love Has Strength Enough to Heal

The angels may have departed, but Joe was now there, comforting and protecting me. The love I felt from him may not have been as powerful as that from the angels or from Christ, but it was marvelous and very comforting nonetheless. The love we share as mortals may be imperfect, but it still has great power to heal and sustain.
Embraced By The Light - page 128

That their hearts might be comforted, being knit together in love . . . Colossians 2:2

Father, the power of love that is in me as a mortal being is a great blessing and responsibility. Teach me to use tenderness and patience as I nurture and develop it within me. Bless me to use love in creating a better home and in strengthening family and all my relationships. May I be a comfort and strength to all.

Affirmation: **The love I share grows and deepens because it is honest and comes from my heart.**

In My Father's House
Are Many Mansions

As our lights merged, I felt as if I had stepped into his countenance, and I felt an utter explosion of love. It was the most unconditional love I have ever felt, and as I saw his arms open to receive me I went to him and received his complete embrace and said over and over, "I'm home. I'm home. I'm finally home." *Embraced By The Light - page 41*

In my Father's house are many mansions: if it were not so, I would have told you. I go to prepare a place for you. And if I go and prepare a place for you, I will come again, and receive you unto myself; that where I am, there ye may be also. And whither I go ye know, and the way ye know. John 14:2-4

Father, thank you for placing your Spirit in my heart as a road map back to my Heavenly Home. Your wisdom is so great that none shall be lost, and all will return back to you.

Affirmation: **I follow my heart which perfectly directs me back to my Heavenly Father.**

July 4

We Are to Pray for One Another's Healing

If the faith of our friends is weak, the strength of our spirits can literally hold them up. If they are sick, our prayers of faith can often give them strength to be healed, unless their illness is appointed as a growing experience. If their death seems near, we must always remember to ask for God's will to be done, otherwise we could frustrate the person making their transition by creating in them a conflict of purpose. The range of our help for others is immense. We can do far more good for our families, friends, or others than we ever imagined.
Embraced By The Light - page 105

Pray one for another, that ye may be healed. The effectual fervent prayer of a righteous man availeth much. James 5:16

Father, thank you for gifting me with the power to heal and bless my family and friends. Remind me always to pray with those who are in poor health. Bless me to pray fervently by joining them in coming to you for your blessings.

Affirmation: **I bless those I love with my greatest gift: the power of my prayer.**

I Must Learn to
Love My Enemies

Not all people are lovable, but when we find someone difficult for us to love, it is often because they remind us of something within ourselves that we don't like. I learned that we must love our enemies— let go of anger, hate, envy, bitterness, and the refusal to forgive. These things destroy the spirit. We will have to account for how we treat others. *Embraced By The Light - pages 51-52*

Love your enemies, bless them that curse you, do good to them that hate you, and pray for them which despitefully use you, and persecute you; That ye may be the children of your Father which is in heaven: for he maketh his sun to rise on the evil and on the good, and sendeth rain on the just and on the unjust. Matthew 5:44-45

Forgive me, Father, for finding it difficult to love those who curse me and hate me. Bless me to look beyond their ill will for me, and to have wisdom to see the underlying pain they carry that sparks their hatred. And bless me to pray for them and forgive them.

Affirmation: **I follow the example of Christ by loving and forgiving even those who hurt me.**

July 6

Spiritual Attributes Are Gifts from God

We were also given the spiritual attributes we would need for our missions, many of them specially designed for our needs . . . and we can continue to learn how to use these abilities or we can choose not to use them at all . . . I saw that we always have the right attribute to help ourselves, though we may not have recognized it or learned how to use it. We need to look within. We need to trust our abilities; the right spiritual tool is always there for us.

Embraced By The Light - page 94

Every man hath his proper gift of God, one after this manner, and another after that. 1 Corinthians 7:7

Father, forgive me when I covet the blessings you grant to my peers. Bless me to honor and hold sacred my own blessings and to use my attributes in ways that best fulfill your purpose for me.

Affirmation: **My attributes are best suited to fulfill my mission in life.**

Seeking Wisdom Opens Doors of Opportunity

*B*y sincerely seeking wisdom, we open ourselves to impressions which can come immediately or at odd moments and provide keys of knowledge which unlock doors of opportunity. *The Ripple Effect - page 95*

I applied mine heart to know, and to search, and to seek out wisdom, and the reason of things . . . *Ecclesiastes 7:25*

*T*hank you, Father. By your power you have filled our universe with intelligence and knowledge of all things. When my heart is open to divine inspirations, you willingly gift me with all that I am prepared to receive. Then you bless me to understand when the time to fulfill its purpose comes. Thank you for your wisdom.

Affirmation: **My heart hungers for greater knowledge of all things, and I willingly release old thoughts for new.**

Prayers with Unconditional Love Are Powerful

I had also watched the "mothers' prayers" and seen that they reached into heaven like bright beacons of light. I knew that the mothers' prayers were the greatest prayers ever heard . . . *The Awakening Heart - page 57*

And she said, O my lord, as thy soul liveth, my lord, I am the woman that stood by thee here, praying unto the Lord. For this child I prayed; and the Lord hath given me my petition which I asked of him . . .
1 Samuel 1:26-27

Thank you, Father, for blessing me as a parent with your loving example. And thank you for directing angels to my aid when I cry out for help for my children. Without your intervention, I would feel lost in my ability to protect them.

Affirmation: **I express unconditional love in my prayers, and I am heard in the heavens.**

Masculine and Feminine Energies Are Balanced in Heaven

Women, too, are in the image of God and are multifaceted. Women's bodies are co-creators of mortal life and this makes us Godlike in a literal sense. In heaven, women and men are perfectly balanced in their roles and are equal. Standing side by side they are perfect complements of each other. *The Ripple Effect - page 6*

Neither is the man without the woman, neither the woman without the man, in the Lord. 1 Corinthians 11:11

Father, I do not completely understand your wisdom for creating differences in male and female roles, so I am often tempted to put down the opposite sex. However, I feel that by demeaning the other role, I am mis-understanding mine. Bless me, Father, with greater knowledge and acceptance, and forgive me for my arrogance. Help me seek to fill my own role in the best way I can.

Affirmation: **I am perfect in my creation and purpose, and I accept the roles that others play.**

Love Is Supreme

"Love one another," Jesus had said. "If you can do that, all else will be fine." Setting an example of love and knowing that no one has the answer for all gave me greater focus and vision for his will in my life.

The Awakening Heart - pages 44-45

Thou shalt love the Lord thy God with all thy heart, and with all thy soul, and with all thy mind . . . Thou shalt love thy neighbour as thyself. On these two commandments hang all the law and the prophets.

Matthew 22:36-40

Father, I often wonder what my mission, my purpose is. Thank you for the knowledge that to love others is the most important reason for my life. Bless me to follow the three most important steps to following your commandments of love, and help me find ways to let love motivate everything I do.

Affirmation: **To love God and then others as myself is my most important mission on earth.**

God Desires Me to Be Diligent in All I Do

*F*ollowing one's heart with passion, direction, and determination is giving life to life . . . God can especially use people who throw themselves passionately into what they love, who walk forward confidently committed to a cause. *The Ripple Effect - page 28*

*T*hou shalt love the Lord thy God with all thy heart, and with all thy soul, and with all thy strength, and with all thy mind . . . *Luke 10:27*

*F*ather, bless me with a heart that feels deeply and a spirit that burns with desire to achieve and excel. I wish to work diligently to use the talents and abilities you created in me. My desire is to honor you with all that I am blessed to be and to have, and to make the most of the life you gave me.

Affirmation: **I embrace my hopes and dreams and pursue them unceasingly.**

Appreciation Opens Doors to Abundance

Gratitude, I have learned, keeps me in tune with my love and appreciation for the abundance of God in my life. When I awake in the morning, I thank God for each new day. I thank him for everything that I have, materially and spiritually . . . I ask him to allow me to expand beyond my narrow-mindedness and self-centeredness, so that I can see the good that comes from everything. *The Awakening Heart - page 218*

In every thing give thanks: for this is the will of God in Christ Jesus concerning you. 1 Thessalonians 5:18

Thank you, Father, for all that I have . . . especially for your love! Keep me grateful to those on earth who bless my life with their love, their service, their talents and gifts. I am truly blessed and thankful!

Affirmation: **I show gratitude and appreciation for the abundance of God in my life.**

Communication with God
Preserves My Life

In my agony I turned to God in prayer, and I found that I could express myself to him. Prayer became my only solace and the life preserver that I clung to. *The Awakening Heart - page 24*

I love the Lord, because he hath heard my voice and my supplications. Because he hath inclined his ear unto me, therefore will I call upon him as long as I live . . . I was brought low, and he helped me. Psalms 116:1-6

Father, when I turn to you with great explanation of my needs, I find you waiting patiently, already knowing my needs, and having already answered my requests. Often, as my life unfolds, I see you providing for needs I do not even know to pray for. Thank you for honoring me with your divine love and presence.

Affirmation: **When I need guidance, I first turn to God in prayer.**

I Receive Glorious Rewards in Loving

We are to love one another. We are to be kind, to be tolerant, to give generous service. I know that greater joy will come to us through love than in any other way. I have seen its wonderful, glorious rewards.
Embraced By The Light - page 147

Brethren . . . be of one mind, live in peace; and the God of love and peace shall be with you. 2 Corinthians 13:11

Father, when I show my love for others, I experience your love for me—and there is no greater gift, no greater joy. Thank you.

Affirmation: **I love and nurture others through heartfelt service, and feel marvelous joy and happiness in their love.**

God Has Power Over All Energies

Within our universe are both positive and negative energies, and both types of energy are essential to creation and growth ... God has absolute power over both energies. Positive energy is just what we would think it is: light, goodness, kindness, love, patience, charity, hope, and so on. And negative energy is just what we would think it is: darkness, hatred, fear (Satan's greatest tool), unkindness, intolerance, selfishness, despair, discouragement, and so on. *Embraced By The Light - page 57*

But the natural man receiveth not the things of the Spirit of God: for they are foolishness unto him: neither can he know them, because they are spiritually discerned. But he that is spiritual judgeth all things, yet he himself is judged of no man. 1 Corinthians 2:14-15

When troubles come, Father, often my spirit wavers and I draw the wrong energy to me. Thank you for being my guiding light and blessing me during times when I am lost.

Affirmation: **My spiritual eyes are open, and I discern which energies are at work in me.**

July 16

God's Glory Shines in the Countenance of Jesus

I saw a pinpoint of light in the distance . . . As I approached it, I noticed the figure of a man standing in it, with the light radiating all around him . . . I saw that the light immediately around him was golden . . . and I could see that the golden halo burst out from around him and spread into a brilliant, magnificent whiteness that extended out for some distance. I felt his light blending into mine, literally, and I felt my light being drawn to his . . . And as our lights merged, I felt as if I had stepped into his countenance, and I felt an utter explosion of love. *Embraced By The Light - pages 40-41*

For God, who commanded the light to shine out of darkness, hath shined in our hearts, to give the light of the knowledge of the glory of God in the face of Jesus Christ. *2 Corinthians 4:6*

Father, as I learn to love, fill me with the light of Jesus. Let it radiate from me and lead others to your greater divine light.

Affirmation: **Because God so loves me, I can draw upon the light and love of Jesus Christ.**

My Prayers
Strengthen Others

*O*ur prayers for others have great strength but can only be answered as far as they do not infringe on the others' free will—or as long as they do not frustrate others' needs. God is bound to let us act for ourselves, but he is also willing to help in any way possible.
Embraced By The Light - page 105

I am the Lord which exercises loving kindness, judgment, and righteousness, in the earth: for in these things I delight, saith the Lord. *Jeremiah 9:24*

*F*ather, sometimes when I pray for others, I pray believing I have perfect solutions for their problems. While I know my heart is in the right place, I am confident and grateful that you will answer according to their needs and your plan for them, not mine. Bless me to always allow for your will whenever I pray in behalf of others.

Affirmation: **I allow for the free will of others in my prayers for God's help in their lives.**

Knowledge of God Precedes Faith in Him

While in the presence of God, I had understood that knowledge and belief precede faith in him. When we learn of God and believe in him, we acquire faith in him. When we experience that faith, it develops further.
The Awakening Heart - page 24

So then faith cometh by hearing, and hearing by the word of God. *Romans 10:17*

Father, thank you for sending your Son, Jesus, to act as your Living Word. Bless me to live within that Word, which is, that you are love and that the only way to come to you is through love. I accept this knowledge with all my heart, and through faith I know that it is true.

Affirmation: **My spirit is open to hear and learn all truth.**

I Trust in the Unseen World of God

$\mathcal{I}$ thought [God] was doing nothing but watch me suffer, when he had already taken care of my needs. Once again I had trusted in what I could see and not in the unseen.
The Awakening Heart - page 64

For we walk by faith, not by sight . . . 2 Corinthians 5:7

Father, forgive me when I cannot see your hand in my life and so question your wisdom or doubt your love and concern for me. Teach me to trust your ability to see my future and know what is best for me. If that is to give me your silence or to let me pass through trials, increase my faith and endurance and my courage to wait upon you. For I know that your loving hand, even when hidden, is over me always. Thank you for teaching me faith in what I cannot see.

Affirmation: **God blesses me in marvelous and unseen ways.**

I Reflect on My Spiritual Needs and Invite My Lord

When I begin to feel the separation or lack of balance between flesh and spirit, I have learned to enter a quiet place within me and reflect on my spiritual needs . . . Then I invite God's presence to enter. As I contemplate that unseen, spiritual part of me, I feel it expand to become the greater part, filled to overflowing with his love. *The Awakening Heart - pages 216-217*

Rejoice the soul of thy servant: for unto thee, O Lord, do I lift up my soul. Psalms 86:4

Father, my soul is empty and dark without the presence of your sweet spirit. Thank you for entering in the moment I invite you. Bless me to always feel your presence and to never doubt that all I need do is desire you.

Affirmation: **I communicate with God from the quiet place within my soul.**

Knowledge of God
Draws Me into Heaven

I was gently drawn up and into a great, whirling, black mass . . . I became aware of other people as well as animals traveling with me, but at a distance. I could not see them, but I sensed that their experience was the same as mine . . . I did sense, however, that there were some who were not moving forward as I, but were lingering in this wonderful blackness. They either didn't have the desire, or simply didn't know how to proceed. But there was no fear. *Embraced By The Light - pages 37-38*

O death, where is thy sting? O grave, where is thy victory? *1 Corinthians 15:55*

In the spirit world, Father, my knowledge of your love will remove me from darkness, and my fears will lose their power to keep me from you. Thank you for my knowledge of Jesus Christ and of the gateway of love that, through his death, he opened for me.

Affirmation: **My knowledge of God draws me close to him now and will draw me to him beyond this life.**

I Let Go of Congestive Forces in My Life

I had learned that one of the greatest skills we can acquire is the ability to let go. To achieve the balance we need, we must let go of the congestive forces in our lives, everything that is weighty or burdensome on our spirits. *The Awakening Heart - page 32*

And Moses' father in law said unto him, The thing that thou doest is not good. Thou wilt surely wear away...for this thing is too heavy for thee; thou art not able to perform it thyself alone. Hearken now unto my voice, I will give thee counsel, and God shall be with thee . . . *Exodus 18:17-19*

Father, thank you for carrying my burdens when they become too heavy for me alone. Your love and understanding have seen me through many tough times. I am learning to recognize what I must discard from my past and am ready now to let go and be free of them. Continue to bless me with your strength and your peace, Father. I love you.

Affirmation: **I counsel with my Heavenly Father, and his Spirit generates confidence and achievement in me.**

My Childhood Established
Foundations to Grow Upon

*L*et us be grateful for our childhoods, even for the negative ones. Let us recognize that life is what it is, and that we are all doing our best. Let us especially be grateful for whatever love we have received. Love is always a gift. We are to praise God for all things. *The Ripple Effect - page 30*

*W*hile I live will I praise the Lord: I will sing praises unto my God while I have any being. *Psalms 146:2*

*T*hank you, Father, for seeing me through difficult times in my childhood, for angels you sent to assist me, and to guide and protect me. Thank you for the experiences that shaped my character and blessed me with greater strength. Help me to accept the things I do not understand, and bless me to rise above them with the knowledge that you allow things for a higher purpose, a greater plan.

Affirmation: **My childhood is in harmony with the mission God sent me to earth to accomplish.**

My Identity Is
Unique in the Eternities

Our greatest identifier is our "presence," and this gives us our uniqueness and sets us apart from anyone else. When we die, our attitudes, demeanor, and personality remain with us. In heaven, who you truly are—your unique identity—is actually sensed by others. There's no need to "get to know you," because you cannot hide yourself. Both who you were at spiritual creation and who you are after creating your life on earth remain with you. *The Ripple Effect - page 5*

I am a stranger in the earth . . . Psalms 119:19

Father, you are truly a Creator beyond compare! Each of your children is wondrously unique with talents and attributes that set us apart. Thank you for making me a co-creator with you by gifting me with power to shape my life here on earth. Help me to build on your original design with love and wisdom, that the person I ultimately become will glorify you forever.

Affirmation: **I create my life to reflect my Creator; I am love and complete with wisdom.**

July 25

To Change,
I Must Desire Change

It was important that I not interfere with the spiritual beliefs of another by imposing my beliefs on them . . . In my zealous desire to be "right" and make others "right" with me, I had impatiently and judgmentally stepped into their path, tripping them, hurting myself, and accomplishing nothing. Now I no longer desired conversion for anyone. I saw that they must desire change for themselves . . . *The Awakening Heart - page 43*

Let us not therefore judge one another any more: but judge this rather, that no man put a stumbling block or an occasion to fall in his brother's way. Romans 14:13

Father, bless me not to wound anyone in their spiritual beliefs. I know that we can only come from our individual perceptions and understandings and that you have already made allowances for that. Remind me should I slip, Father, that you are in control. Place deep within my heart the need to be loving over the need to be "right."

Affirmation: **I am a stepping stone for others, and my love encourages their faith.**

I Am a Child of Light and Loved by My Heavenly Father

We are here to have love for every person born on earth. Their earthly form might be black, yellow, brown, handsome, ugly, thin, fat, wealthy, poor, intelligent, or ignorant, but we are not to judge by these appearances. Each spirit has the capacity to be filled with love and eternal energy. *Embraced By The Light - page 51*

Ye are all the children of light . . . be patient toward all men. See that none render evil . . . unto any man; but ever follow that which is good, both among yourselves, and to all men. 1 Thessalonians 5:5, 14-15

How grateful I am, Father, for the variety of people in life. To see beauty and obtain joy from all your creation is to witness your versatility, your perfect multifaceted spirit. Thank you for blessing us all.

Affirmation: **I embrace all God's children, and I experience the versatility in his love.**

I Seek Total Harmony with My Creator

To become as perfect as a mortal being can become, we need to bring the mind, body, and spirit into total harmony. To become perfect in the spirit, we must add to that harmony Christ-like love and righteousness.
Embraced By The Light - pages 56-57

Let not sin therefore reign in your mortal body, that ye should obey it in the lusts thereof. *Romans 6:12*

Forgive me, Father, when my flesh is weak and my spirit is not in harmony with you. My emotions sometimes take hold, and I find myself down paths that are difficult to return from, not knowing what directed me there. Bless me to become more aware, to examine my thoughts and feelings and keep them pure. Help me also to control my body's appetites and passions, to balance them with my spirit. Keep me mindful at all times to become as you are: perfect in mind, body and spirit.

Affirmation: **My spirit is in harmony with God, and my mind and body reflect this.**

Patience Is a Natural Attribute of the Father in Heaven

*I*n the spirit world no one is made to feel uncomfortable by being forced to do or accept things for which they are not prepared. Patience is a natural attribute there. *Embraced By The Light - page 72*

*N*ow the Lord is that Spirit: and where the Spirit of the Lord is, there is liberty. 2 *Corinthians 3:17*

Father, your gentle persuasion and patience brought me to pursue your love, when force might have turned me away. Thank you for patiently waiting for me to come to you and for understanding when I was not ready. Bless me with a calm and patient spirit as I continue growing in the freedom of your love and grace. I am stronger in my ability to choose when I am patient to act. Make me as patient and loving as you in guiding others toward change.

Affirmation: **Patience is a natural attribute of my spirit. I am peaceful, calm and serene.**

July 29

My Soul Mates
Help Serve God's Purpose

We chose to come to earth with certain others because of the work we would do together. Some of us wanted to unite in a cause to change certain things on earth, and we could best do it with certain circumstances brought about by selected parents or others.
Embraced By The Light - pages 92-93

The soul of Jonathan was knit with the soul of David, and Jonathan loved him as his own soul. 1 Samuel 18:1

Father, thank you for blessing me with kindred friends and family to travel life's journey with. As we unite to fulfill your will, bless us with understanding of our purpose together. Be with us in our service, and give us wisdom to work through our difficulties. Help us, Father, to honor you by completing all tasks that we committed in heaven to do on earth.

Affirmation: **I share circumstances on earth with my soul mates from heaven.**

Unsettled Souls Are Drawn to Their Past

When our souls are unsettled, subconsciously we draw to our lives the kinds of experiences and relationships we have had in the past. We do this in order to relive them, to make sense of them, to attempt to make them work for us—this time. It happens again and again, and until we understand the truth behind our circumstances, the cycle of failure continues. *The Ripple Effect - page 146*

Therefore if any man be in Christ, he is a new creature: old things are passed away; behold, all things are become new. 2 Corinthians 5:17

Father, please help me to find peace with my past, to make sense of my choices by finding some degree of the truth behind them. Bless me to free myself from the pain and sorrow they have caused me and others, and may I learn from the lessons my wrong choices taught me. Help me to create a new future for myself and to stop the cycle of failure and disappointment in my life. And thank you, Father, for clearing a way for me to do this.

Affirmation: **I am a new creature in Christ, my life brand new and just beginning.**

July 31

Finding Balance Is a Fundamental Law

I believed that I could not live in . . . the world in which I currently lived. Now I saw that I was so involved in what I had once experienced that not only was I out of balance, I was breaking a fundamental law of health. I was trapped in spiritual gluttony.

The Awakening Heart - page 32

Be content with such things as ye have: for he hath said, I will never leave thee, nor forsake thee.

Hebrews 13:5

Father, keep me balanced in both the physical and spiritual energies of my heart. Bless me not to swing too far towards one or the other, but to live the law of balance that governs my mortality and come to understand it. When I become trapped either way, encourage me in breaking habits that hold power over me. Bless me to discover new goals and strengths within to decrease the strong desires pulling me in both directions. Thank you for this opportunity to strengthen my spirit.

Affirmation: **I have power and knowledge to overcome my appetites. I know that what I do not feed cannot grow.**

August 1

God's Love Ends Cycles of Guilt and Fear

$\mathcal{I}$ saw the evil in surrendering to one of Satan's greatest tools—my personal cycles of guilt and fear. I understood that I had to let go of the past. If I had broken laws or sinned, I needed to change my heart, forgive myself, and then move onward. If I had hurt someone, I needed to start loving them—honestly—and seek their forgiveness. If I had damaged my own spirit, I needed to approach God and feel his love again—his healing love. *Embraced By The Light - pages 69-70*

There is no fear in love; but perfect love casteth out fear: because fear hath torment. He that feareth is not made perfect in love. 1 John 4:18

Father, it is easy to lay claim to fear and guilt when all my life I have been programmed to do so. Help me to remember that love and fear cannot co-exist, and that I must let go of fear to fully claim your love. Thank you for not counting my sins, but instead, blessing me through them.

Affirmation: **I am perfectly safe in the loving arms of God.**

My Beliefs Help Me Reach My Highest Potential

Our beliefs can hold the spirit back from reaching its greatest potential if they inhibit the love that we naturally want to share . . . We can let go of our impure mortal belief systems by seeking our spiritual selves in our Creator, our Father in Heaven.
The Awakening Heart - pages 51-52

But we are bound to give thanks always to God for you, brethren beloved of the Lord, because God hath from the beginning chosen you to salvation through sanctification of the Spirit and belief of the truth . . . 2 Thessalonians 2:13

Father, it is hard for me to move beyond my belief system to include new insight I feel your Spirit teaching. Bless me with courage to venture out of my established boundaries and to find you in greater abundance. Bring me to the truth that my soul so yearns for. And thank you for choosing me to receive salvation.

Affirmation: **I give thanks to my Creator, and he blesses me in all my needs, and gifts me with an ability to reach my greatest potential.**

I Rely on God Alone to Guide My Future

Because [mediums and channelers] only "see" what has already been filtered through our conscious or subconscious minds, their readings can be based on deceptive input and therefore is not useful to them or us. We can acquire more honest guidance by seeking our answers from God, asking him to place the truth into our hearts.

The Awakening Heart - page 51

Only the Lord give thee wisdom and understanding . . . Then shalt thou prosper . . . 1 Chronicles 22:12-13

Father, it excites and comforts me to know that no one stands between you and me. I can take my concerns directly to you and receive direct answers and guidance in return. Help me seek truth in the purest, most direct way, with an open heart, and relying on my spirit's closeness to you. Help me know myself well enough to discern between your guidance and my own desires.

Affirmation: **I turn to God for the knowledge and wisdom I need each day.**

Service Is a Healing Balm to My Entire Being

We are at our most self-centered state when we are depressed. Nothing can sap our natural strength and health as much as prolonged depression. But when we make the effort to move ourselves away from self and begin to concentrate on the needs of others and how to serve them, we begin to heal. Service is a balm to both the spirit and body. *Embraced By The Light - page 63*

Heaviness in the heart of man maketh it stoop: but a good word maketh it glad. Proverbs 12:25

Father, forgive me when I selfishly focus on my needs and shut out the needs of others. Bless me to break away from self-pity and negative thinking by showing me how to serve and lift those around me. Thank you, Father, for blessing me with knowledge that service to others brings happiness and joy and healing to the soul.

Affirmation: **I love to be in the service of others; each contact blesses me with great joy and happiness.**

Heavenly Father Never Abandons Me

The awakening of my spirit, although exciting, was an isolating force. While it led me to the spiritual being within me and brought me closer to God, it also separated me from those with whom I had once shared similar views. *The Awakening Heart - page 48*

Ye shall be scattered, every man to his own, and shall leave me alone: and yet I am not alone, because the Father is with me. John 16:32

Father, your understanding of my life brings me closer to you each day. I know that your Spirit senses when to draw me close or when to let me come to you on my own. Thank you for your loving grace and wisdom.

Affirmation: **My life holds within it all that I need, and I am satisfied being alone with my God.**

The Extent of God's Love Is Marvelous to Me

To say that the fires of hell will claim anyone forever is to deny the extent of God's love, of his understanding, and of his willingness to forgive. We doubt his judgment in the first place if we believe he would send us here, block us from heaven, and then expect us to return to him un-blemished. *The Ripple Effect - page 89*

They shall all know me, from the least of them unto the greatest of them, saith the Lord: for I will forgive their iniquity, and I will remember their sin no more.
Jeremiah 31:34

Father, your unconditional love defines your forgiveness. It is a priceless gift, especially when I consider how many times I have not followed your will for me. It comforts me to know that, instead of wanting to punish me and push me farther away, you want me to learn from my mistakes and grow closer to you. Help me to remember that when I limit your love through my fear or guilt, I also limit my own power to heal and to love.

Affirmation: **God's unlimited love allows forgiveness for all my sins.**

August 7

I Realize My Greatest Potential by Living the Father's Will

We can endure in this life because [God] is with us, caring for us, helping us to realize our potential. Asking for his help is a sign of strength that our spirit wants to live. Asking for his will to be done is a sign that our spirits want to live in him again. *The Ripple Effect - page 207*

Humble yourselves therefore under the mighty hand of God, that he may exalt you in due time: Casting all your care upon him; for he careth for you. 1 Peter 5:6-7

Father, help me reach my greatest potential by keeping me close to you so that I follow your will. Bless me to trust your faith in me and to stretch beyond my usual reach to accomplish your goals for me. And thank you for setting my standards high and for blessing me with the right opportunities and all the necessary skills to successfully meet them.

Affirmation: **I humbly place my cares in the mighty hands of God, and his Spirit never fails me.**

I Must Be True to My Spirit that Came from God

*I*f we want to grow to become all that we can be, we must be true to ourselves—to the spirit within us that came from heaven. However, knowing ourselves requires painful effort, and this is the test. *The Ripple Effect - page 3*

*E*xamine yourselves, whether ye be in the faith; prove your own selves. Know ye not your own selves, how that Jesus Christ is in you . . . *2 Corinthians 13:5*

*F*ather, help me to examine my spirit and to use wisdom as I look for my worth. My spirit hungers to honor you by being Christlike, and yet I know that I have often failed. Thank you for bringing me to know myself. By your tests of my faith, I am more fully aware of my value and of what I must change. Remind me when I forget that my spirit's strong desire is to fulfill its purpose, and guide me to serve you, Father.

Affirmation: **I am true to myself and to my God.**

August 9

God Prompts Me to
Keep a Willing Heart

There is nothing wrong with not knowing our missions. We are not always meant to know. Some people seem preoccupied with trying to figure out their mission and they waste valuable time. Instead, they should live into their purpose by following their hearts. I was told it is best to follow God's promptings, to be flexible and moldable. He can make better use of our lives that way.
The Ripple Effect - pages 20-21

Whosoever is of a willing heart, let him bring it, an offering of the Lord... Exodus 35:5

Father, help me to know the difference between the promptings of my heart which are connected to your Spirit, and the promptings of my heart which are connected to my own desires. Keep me open to your will, and teach me the grace of walking in your footsteps.

Affirmation: **I place my willing heart into the loving hands of my Lord.**

Angels Strengthen Me with Loving Support

When the heavens scrolled back, I saw the earth with its billions of people on it. I saw them scrambling for existence, making mistakes, experiencing kindness, finding love, grieving for death, and I saw the angels hovering above them. The angels knew the people by name and watched over them closely. They cheered when good was done and were saddened by mistakes. They hovered about to help and give direction and protection. *The Ripple Effect - page 121*

And there appeared an angel unto him from heaven, strengthening him. *Luke 22:43*

Father, thank you for blessing me with the loving spirit of angels who comfort and support me when I need them. I know the angels are made happy when I do good, and saddened by my mistakes. I also know they do not judge me but are attentive and caring. Help me to show them my gratitude by having loving thoughts and by doing kind deeds that will bring them joy.

Affirmation: **Angels sing and rejoice to see my love for the Father and my will to do good.**

August 11

Jesus' Life Teaches Me About Love

*B*ecause of his love for us, Jesus revealed the keys by which we may unlock the love which exists within us. If we truly love God with all our hearts and souls, we will pattern our lives after his words. As we live the universal laws he has taught us, we will grow in light and strength. *The Ripple Effect - pages 153-154*

*A*nd this commandment have we from him, That he who loveth God love his brother also. *1 John 4:21*

*F*ather, the more I learn about Jesus, the greater is my love for you and for all people. Thank you for helping me understand the magnificent power of his love. I am learning to love without condition and to express my love in more Christ-like ways. Bless me as I continue to grow, and thank you for opportunities.

Affirmation: **I am learning to love unconditionally and pattern myself after Christ.**

August 12

Jesus Shepherds Me and Draws Me Near

As I saw his arms open to receive me I went to him and received his complete embrace and . . . I felt his enormous spirit and knew that I had always been a part of him, that in reality I had never been away from him. *Embraced By The Light - page 41*

And, lo, I am with you alway, even unto the end of the world. Matthew 28:20

Thank you, Father, for prompting me to remember my brother, Jesus Christ. Thank you for the unity of his spirit with mine which has its foundation in your love. Bless me to always bear witness of his spirit and of his love for all mankind.

Affirmation: **I am blessed with knowledge of Jesus and know his spirit is always with me.**

The Sacrifice of Jesus Is My Key for Returning Home

*J*esus is known by many names around the world, but what we call him is not as important as what he represents, especially in the sacrifice he made to bring us home to our Father. *The Ripple Effect - pages109-110*

*F*or God so loved the world, that he gave his only begotten Son, that whosoever believeth in him should not perish, but have everlasting life. *John 3:16*

*F*ather, thank you for the plan of salvation and for Jesus Christ, who so willingly gave his life to return me to you. Thank you for sending your message to the world through him, and for blessing us to know that our path back home is paved with love.

Affirmation: **Through the sacrifice of love, I will return home to my Heavenly Father.**

God Wants Me Clean from Past Mistakes

I was shown that gluttony is a sin and that it can involve more than just food. Gluttony of anything, including our dwelling on the past and the mistakes we made there, can enslave us. The would haves, should haves, and could haves are all ties to the past, and they can bind us unless we let them go. *The Awakening Heart - pages 32-33*

If a man therefore purge himself from these, he shall be a vessel unto honour, sanctified, and meet for the master's use, and prepared unto every good work. *2 Timothy 2:21*

Father, forgive me for holding on to would haves, should haves, and could haves from my past. They are difficult to let go because they are what I know. Help me to let go of them and to trust in my future by trusting more in you and in your desires for me. Bless me to move onward and become a more perfect vessel for your use.

Affirmation: **My earthly vessel is cleansed, and I receive the rewards my Father in Heaven wills to give me.**

My Spirit Matures by Gaining Understanding

The mortal body ages through time in hours, days, and years. But the spirit quickens or matures through its understanding and ability to master tasks required of it. In heaven a being's maturity isn't segmented into periods of time. *The Ripple Effect - page 7*

For to one is given by the Spirit the word of wisdom; to another the word of knowledge . . . to another faith . . . to another the gifts of healing . . . 1 Corinthians 12:8-9

Father, so many areas of my life are measured by time that I easily forget that I am an eternal being. Help me to remember that I am not here merely to pass a determined number of years but to accomplish a number of tasks that lie along my path. I am grateful for the opportunities to grow that this world offers, and for the gifts you have provided to aid me. Help me maintain a focus which is eternal, so that I may achieve the spiritual goals you and I established long before I began my physical life.

Affirmation: **My spirit is evolving and maturing through understanding and knowledge.**

 *August 16*

I Make Mistakes Because I Am Growing in Spirit

When we fall down, we need to get up, dust ourselves off, and get moving again. If we fall down again, even a million times, we still need to keep going; we're growing more than we think. In the spirit world they don't see sin as we do here. All experiences can be positive. All are learning experiences. *Embraced By The Light - page 70*

When I fall, I shall arise; when I sit in darkness, the Lord shall be a light unto me. *Micah 7:8*

Father, thank you for being there to lift me up and strengthen me the many times when I have fallen and failed. And thank you for lighting my way when my life is dark and I have nothing but a sense of your love to keep me going. Bless me to internalize the knowledge that you love me unconditionally—no matter what! This understanding brings me the strength I need to pick myself up when I fall. Your love increases my desire to move ahead and make the changes my life needs.

Affirmation: **With God's help, my spirit finds growth in failure and strength in moving on again.**

August 17

My Cells Are
Blessed with Memory

Each of us . . . carries in our presence an energy "blueprint" that contains our present thoughts, deeds, and experiences, as well as all of our background and possible future . . . The pure truth of everything exists within our cells and our spirit.
The Awakening Heart - page 50

I will praise thee; for I am fearfully and wonderfully made: marvelous are thy works; and that my soul knoweth right well. Psalms 139:14

Father, thank you for my physical body with its perfect blueprint. Everything necessary for me and my posterity is stored within us. All that I am, my children and my children's children can become. My thoughts, my deeds, my experiences are an inheritance to aid them in their growth. Your plan is perfect, Father.

Affirmation: **My gifts as a mortal being stem from beyond this world to the Creator who wondrously made me.**

God Is Awakening Me to My Higher Calling

Sometimes our Heavenly Father allows things into our lives just to awaken us to a higher calling. The passion we feel about a matter might be the first clue that the job was ours all along. When we need to be brought to an understanding, the recognition of a need does just that. *The Ripple Effect - page 234*

This one thing I do, forgetting those things which are behind, and reaching forth unto those things which are before, I press toward the mark for the prize of the high calling of God in Christ Jesus. Philippians 3:13-14

Thank you, Father, for assigning me the passion and desire to bring about your glory by doing your will. Help me recognize opportunities or needs in others which spark a desire in me to be of service. Then help me move swiftly and with determination to fill them, drawing upon the unique abilities gifted to me by you. Bless me to then stay open to hearing your voice, should you call me to serve in a different way.

Affirmation: **I am steadfast and committed in the work God calls me to.**

August 19

My Words Have
Power to Create

$\mathcal{I}$ was shown that many of the illnesses of my life were the result of depression or feelings of not being loved. I saw that I had often yielded to negative "self-talk," such as "Oh, my aches and pains," "I'm not loved," "Look at my sufferings," "I can't endure this," and more . . . I opened the door and accepted them as mine. My body then lived a sort of self-fulfilling prophecy: "Woe is me," was translated in the body as "I am sick." *Embraced By The Light - page 64*

Who so keepeth his mouth and his tongue keepeth his soul from troubles. Proverbs 21:23

Thank you, Father, for giving me creative power over my life. Teach me to use the power of my thoughts and the strength of my tongue appropriately. Let my mouth speak only words which bless and heal and spread your light and love.

Affirmation: **My thoughts and words strengthen my health, lift my spirits, and give me life.**

Life's Purpose Is to Bring Me Closer to God

In life we don't remember. We cannot hear, see, or physically feel God. We act blindly and perhaps our true colors or our true ignorance comes out. These revelations about ourselves teach us what we need to work on to become more like God, and he kindly gives us the time and space to work on them. No purpose of life is given to force us from God. *The Ripple Effect - page 89*

For the Lord thy God is a merciful God; he will not forsake thee, neither destroy thee . . . Deuteronomy 4:31

Father, as I walk in faith, sometimes faltering and often triumphing, my awareness of how much I want to serve you grows. I dream of my return back "home," and I hope to return there with honor. Bless me to become more aware of the quality and consequences of my choices. And help me always to remember that you forgive me when I choose imperfectly.

Affirmation: **I embrace the knowledge I gain of myself, and it helps me draw nearer to Heavenly Father.**

With Jesus as the Light, There Is No Darkness

$\mathscr{I}$ was filled with wonder that I had actually visited with the Savior of the world and been held in his arms. I began to feel stronger as I reflected on the knowledge I had received while in his presence, and I knew his light would continue to give me strength and comfort in hours of need.
Embraced By The Light - pages 125-126

The Lord is my light and my salvation; whom shall I fear . . . Psalms 27:1

Father, as a mortal being I look for heroes to emulate, to image myself after, to set a standard. Thank you for sending me the perfect hero in your Son, Jesus Christ. In him is every attribute I desire to duplicate in myself.

Affirmation: **Jesus is my mentor. I emulate him and follow him towards perfection.**

I Embrace Every Moment of My Life

Every encounter we have, even if brief and seemingly unimportant, may have more significance than we know. A brief encounter may begin a greater ripple that reaches its intended purpose years later. Everyone who comes into our lives may be part of our mission, and we, a part of theirs . . . By being positive and helpful towards others, even in casual moments, we can make the most of our time on earth. *The Ripple Effect - page 19*

And thou shalt rejoice in every good thing which the Lord thy God hath given unto thee, and unto thine house . . . and the stranger that is among you. Deuteronomy 26:11

Father, your ways reflect greater love and charity than my own. Bless me to be more like you, watching for even the smallest ways to be thoughtful and kind. Help me to embrace each moment I am blessed with, to let no opportunity slip by for showing my compassion and respect to those around me.

Affirmation: **My every choice and action is inspired by my desire to do good and to uplift those around me.**

August 23

Many Are Called to Feed the Lord's Sheep

We are all shepherds to some degree. We are all compelled by the spirit to seek his truth and do his will, each in our own way, creating waves that overlap others and resonate within their souls, inviting them to do better, to look to God, to live life to the fullest with joy. *The Ripple Effect - page xv*

And let us consider one another to provoke unto love and to good works . . . Hebrews 10:24

Father, I am grateful for the amazing opportunity to be your disciple and to share the truths that have brought my life such happiness. Make constant my desire to spread the good news of your everlasting joy, and help me to inspire and support others in their efforts to do the same.

Affirmation: **I share the happiness I have found with a full heart, that others may know truth.**

To Listen Is a Part of Prayer

*A*s one prays and listens, the life-giving words of the Creator enter the soul. It is one thing to pray, it is another to listen to the answer. *The Ripple Effect - page 104*

*H*ear instruction, and be wise, and refuse it not. Blessed is the man that heareth me, watching daily at my gates, waiting at the posts of my doors. *Proverbs 8:33-34*

*F*ather, bless me to be still and quiet in moments of prayer, to wait upon the calming direction of your spirit in answer to my requests. Bless me with patience to give time, energy and reverence to listening for your voice. And give me courage to act upon what you show me without doubt or reluctance.

Affirmation: **In reverence and humility I listen for God's voice, which quickens my spirit.**

My Service Shows Love for Others

I needed to let go of the past by creating love here and now in my life and in the world I now lived in. I vowed to change my sick spirit by doing service, having faith, and sharing love, the acts that I had been shown are among the reasons God placed us here.

The Awakening Heart - page 33

If thou draw out thy soul to the hungry and satisfy the afflicted soul; then shall thy light rise . . .

Isaiah 58:10

Father, bless me to know how to serve those that are homeless, in need of shelter, clothing or food. Open my spirit to see the best uses in service for my time and my resources. Bring me to know whether to serve personally or to donate to charities and community efforts. No matter how you choose I should give, Father, bless me to do so with a willing and loving heart. Most of all, bless me to never waiver in sharing my knowledge of truths which can give spiritual nourishment to hungering hearts and thirsting spirits.

Affirmation: **My heart is directed by God and his will for how I can best serve.**

August 26

My Mistakes Teach Me
Valuable Lessons

*A*ctually, *nothing* is in vain if we learn from it. Every negative experience can be turned to our benefit when we humbly learn from our mistakes. We can always change and move on. For many, though, anxiety saps life from their souls. *The Ripple Effect - page 78*

*B*e not overcome of evil, but overcome evil with good. *Romans 12:21*

*F*ather, give me the wisdom to look for the contradictions in my life that hinder my spiritual development. When I move off course, help me to understand what drew me there, so I will become aware of my deeper needs and learn to serve them in a more righteous way. Bless me as I rectify and balance my motivations and desires, and bring me to strengthen my spirit as I use my creative energy to change my circumstances.

Affirmation: **I am teachable and I conquer my trials and challenges .**

Heavenly Father Is Just and Fair

I thought that we had to nag the Lord and to continue nagging him until something happened . . . I would resort to bribing . . . bargaining . . . in desperation, I would beg, and then, when all else failed, I would throw a tantrum . . . Now I understood that my prayers had been demonstrations of . . . my lack of faith in his willingness to answer me based on the merits of my needs alone. I doubted that he was fair or even able . . . All these doubts created a barrier between me and God. *Embraced By The Light - pages 105-106*

What things so ever ye desire, when ye pray, believe that ye receive them, and ye shall have them. Mark 11:24

Father, forgive me for doubting your interest in me and your ability to understand my needs. Bless me with confidence when I pray, to never doubt and to know that you do hear my prayers. Thank you for your patience and understanding as I develop more in you.

Affirmation: **My prayers of confidence demonstrate my faith, and God blesses me according to my needs.**

My Spirit Is
Limitless and Free

Then I felt a surge of energy. It was almost as if I felt a pop or release inside me, and my spirit was suddenly drawn out through my chest and pulled upward, as if by a giant magnet. My first impression was that I was free. There was nothing unnatural about the experience. I was above the bed, hovering near the ceiling. My sense of freedom was limitless and it seemed as if I had done this forever. *Embraced By The Light - page 29*

I knew a man in Christ . . . (whether in the body, I cannot tell; or out of the body, I cannot tell: God knoweth) such an one caught up to the third heaven . . . and heard unspeakable words, which it is not lawful for a man to utter. 2 Corinthians 12:2-4

Draw me ever near to you, Father. Remind me often that I am divine and that my true self is one with you. When I am released from this body of clay, may my spirit rise in freedom to be with you, to travel the universe, and to glory in all your creation again.

Affirmation: **My spirit is one with my Creator.**

August 29

I Am Blessed with
Eternal Progression

*E*ach of us, I was told, is at a different level of spiritual development and understanding . . . As an individual raises his level of understanding about God and his own eternal progress, he might feel discontented with the teachings of his present church and seek a different philosophy or religion to fill that void. When this occurs he has reached another level of understanding and will long for further truth and knowledge, and for another opportunity to grow. *Embraced By The Light - pages 45-46*

*A*nd I will give you pastors according to mine heart, which shall feed you with knowledge and understanding. *Jeremiah 3:15*

*F*ather, I am grateful for the level of knowledge and truth I have been blessed to achieve. Help me to examine my beliefs, to test their soundness and their purity in truth. Bless me to continue in my growth and to seek your ways through your appointed servants. Help me to trust my spirit to find your truths wherever I must seek them.

Affirmation: **I find spiritual progress in God's will for me.**

August 30

I Have Eternal Friendships

We have all had the experience of meeting someone whose spirit we recognize without quite knowing what to make of it. We know them. They know us. We recognize each other's souls when we look into each other's eyes and heart. When that happens, we may actually be recognizing that we knew each other before we ever came to this earth. *The Awakening Heart - page 151*

And it came to pass, that, when Elisabeth heard the salutation of Mary, the babe leaped in her womb; and Elisabeth . . . spake . . . and said, lo, as soon as the voice of thy salutation sounded in mine ears, the babe leaped in my womb for joy. Luke 1:41-44

Father, thank you for blessing me with precious and eternal friendships that carry a love so deep it is everlasting. Bless these, and all my relationships, present and future, that their purposes be fulfilled in you.

Affirmation: **My friendships are forever, extending beyond this lifetime into the eternities.**

My Spirit Accepted the Challenge to Assist Others

Our spirits remember. They remember that we make decisions in heaven by different standards than we do on earth . . . Our spirits remember that we volunteered to come into our present conditions, not only to learn and to help ourselves, but to teach and to help others as well. *The Ripple Effect - page 37*

Ye also are full of goodness, filled with all knowledge, able also to admonish one another. Romans 15:14

Thank you, Father, for the opportunity to come into this world to live by faith and to gain experience so that my spirit may add new knowledge to that which it already has. Help me receive new truth with gratitude, always willing to teach others. Instruct me to use my abilities as a confident mentor to bless those in need of my assistance.

Affirmation: **I offer my knowledge and abilities so that others may also come to God.**

Heaven Speaks the Language of the Heart

*O*ur communication was nonverbal, all thoughts and feelings that we chose to express were expressed directly, straight from his heart to mine and vice versa. *The Awakening Heart - page 15*

*H*is word was in mine heart as a burning fire... *Jeremiah 20:9*

*F*ather, your love radiates purity and comes straight from your heart into mine. Thank you for blessing me to experience its deep, rich expression of warmth. Help me remember that you have created me after the likeness of that which is spiritual and have gifted me with like abilities to communicate from my heart. Bless me with a burning desire to develop a more direct communication with you and with those I love. Let my love be felt and expressed from my heart.

Affirmation: **My thoughts and emotions rise above the physical, as I express them from my heart.**

September 2

Redemption Includes All God's Children

We must not think in black and white, but more like God thinks, without limiting any possibility for love and redemption. We should try everyday to see the good in people as he sees it. Not that we should blindly trust all people, but we can temper our judgment with the recognition that a piece of God dwells in each person, which is always redeemable. *The Ripple Effect - page 89*

There is no difference between the Jew and the Greek: for the same Lord over all is rich unto all that call upon him. For whosoever shall call upon the name of the Lord shall be saved. Romans 10:12-13

Father, how blind is our world of religion in its jealous attempts to harness and possess exclusively your love and redemption. The Scriptures say that whosoever believeth in you will not be ashamed. Jesus taught that we are to share the gospel of peace and bring glad tidings of good things to all who will listen. Bless us, Father, as we live in diverse and separate faiths. Bring us together with understanding that your love is for us all.

Affirmation: **God's love and grace is unlimited.**

September 3

The Power of Love Holds the Universe in Place

To learn to love more fully is the reason we have come to earth. Love is the energy which holds the universe in place. It is the gateway through which we return to our Creator. It can conquer any problem, ease any suffering, heal any disease. Love creates and magnifies the joys of life. And, at the moment of death, love turns all earthly pain into indescribable bliss. *The Ripple Effect - page 144*

Charity beareth all things, believeth all things, hopeth all things, endureth all things. Charity never faileth . . . 1 Corinthians 13:7-8

Thank you, Father. You are the personification of love, and all that you are is unmistakable in your creation. The world and the stars are wondrous miracles, but never so great as the love and grace you show me by saving and cleansing my soul. Bless me, Father, to meditate on the glory of this and to comprehend your magnificence.

Affirmation: **The glory of God is expressed in all his creations, including me.**

September 4

I Heal My Body by Verbalizing Remedies

*P*ositive self-talk begins the healing process. Once we have identified the illness or problem, we need to start verbalizing its remedy. We need to remove thoughts of the illness from our minds and begin concentrating on its cure. Then we need to verbalize this cure, letting our words add to the power of our thoughts. This creates an excitement in the intelligences around us, and they then go into motion, working to heal us. I understood that this verbalization can best be done in prayer. *Embraced By The Light - page 65*

*A*nd all things, whatsoever ye shall ask in prayer, believing, ye shall receive. *Matthew 21:22*

*F*ather, bless my body with the strength it needs to fulfill my mission on earth. And bless me to be in touch with it, to listen when it signals that something needs change. Help me examine my words for indicators that my illness is not my own creation.

Affirmation: **I verbalize in prayer the remedy to my needs, and healing energy comes immediately to my aid.**

September 5

The Purity of My Soul
Lights My Countenance

*O*ur auras, or countenances, display the feelings and emotions of our souls. God sees them, angels see them, and Satan sees them. Even very sensitive people here can see them. We can protect ourselves by controlling our thoughts, by allowing the light of Christ to enter our lives. As we do this, the light of Christ will shine through us and will actually appear in our countenances. *Embraced By The Light - pages 91-92*

*F*or ye were sometimes darkness, but now are ye light in the Lord; walk as children of light . . . *Ephesians 5:8*

*F*ather, because you hold me close in the countenance of your love, I feel my spirit grow in brilliance and in love. Thank you for sharing your light while allowing me to grow. Bless me to control my emotions and to display the light of Christ within me.

Affirmation: **I am a child of light and my countenance radiates the energy of Christ-like love.**

My Creator Knows When to Intervene in My Life

Sometimes God plays an active role in preventing accidents or injuries that in his divine wisdom would not be for our good. In these cases, perhaps our knowing about his intervention creates the very growth . . . we . . . need. Although we have forgotten that we chose our path beforehand, God has not forgotten. He is an active partner in helping us stay on the path which holds the experiences we need for growth.

The Ripple Effect - page 126

He delivereth and rescueth, and he worketh signs and wonders in heaven and in earth, who hath delivered Daniel from the power of the lions.

Daniel 6:27

Father, thank you for being intimately involved in my life. I know your divine direction brings to my path what is necessary for my spiritual development. I see your hand evident in my life and am reminded of your constant presence and love.

Affirmation: **Under God's close care, I successfully fulfill my mission.**

September 7

I Am Learning to Love as Christ Taught

*J*esus didn't say to love those who think as we do, or to love those we trust, or to love those who love us. He said to love one another even as he has loved us. His love is the most honest, pure, and unconditional love we can know. He loves the murderer, the rapist, the thief, the liar and yes, the abortionist, the same as he loves you or me. He loves the sick, the weak, the lost, and the ignorant as he does the healthy, the strong, the saved, and the learned. *The Ripple Effect - page 43*

*A*nd the Lord make you to increase and abound in love one toward another, and toward all men . . . *1 Thessalonians 3:12*

*F*ather, thank you for the example of Jesus' love. Bless me to love unconditionally as he loves. And help me learn to trust while opening myself to love, knowing that your Spirit will guard me and show me the way.

*A*ffirmation: **My greatest attribute is my love for my Creator and for my fellow man.**

September 8

God Promises I Will Not Suffer More Than I Can Bear

We are never alone in any trial of suffering, and we will not be allowed to suffer more than we can bear. This is a promise from God. He and his angels surround us, love us, and help us choose the path of greatest spiritual growth. It is his will that we overcome the world and find joy and happiness in our lives. *The Ripple Effect - page 59*

These things I have spoken unto you, that in me ye might have peace. In the world ye shall have tribulation: but be of good cheer; I have overcome the world. John 16:33

Thank you, Father, I am comforted to know that, even in my toughest trials, you bless me with strength to endure and overcome as Jesus did. With your constant love and support, I will follow in the steps of Jesus, finding peace through every hardship.

Affirmation: **I am victorious in tribulation and find joy and happiness in my life.**

My Spirit Is Receptive to God

I was truly beginning to understand the power of the spirit over the body . . . I knew that my mind created my thoughts, and my body performed my actions, but the spirit had been a mystery to me. Now I understood that the spirit is a mystery to most people. I saw that it functions, generally, without the mind even being aware of it. The spirit communicates with God, being the receptive device that receives knowledge and insight from him . . . *Embraced By The Light - page 66*

The spirit of man is the candle of the Lord, searching all the inward parts... Proverbs 20:27

Father, make me more aware that my spirit receives your guiding influence. Help me recognize and follow its gentle tugging that leads me to fulfill what I promised to do— which is to glorify you with my life on earth.

Affirmation: **My spirit receives and rejoices in the will of God, my Father.**

The Chosen Savior of This World Is Jesus

I understood that he was the Son of God, though he himself was also a God, and that he had chosen from before the creation of the world to be our Savior . . . This knowledge was more like remembering. Things were coming back to me from long before my life on earth, things that had been purposely blocked from me by a "veil" of forgetfulness at my birth. *Embraced By The Light - page 44*

But with the precious blood of Christ, as of a lamb without blemish and without spot: Who verily was foreordained before the foundation of the world . . . *1 Peter 1:19-20*

Father, your knowledge of the world and how to overcome it through the sacrifice of Jesus has blessed the world and saved it from ignorance. My life is blessed because Jesus taught your perfect love, and when I live his teachings by faith, I come nearer to you. Thank you for your wisdom and love in sending Jesus. Help me listen and hear my own heart's witness that he lives for me.

Affirmation: **My spirit recognizes Jesus as the Savior of this world, and rejoices in his sacrifice for me.**

 September 11

My Circumstances
Lead Me to God

*H*eavenly Father uses the tool of circumstances to lead us to him. Some believe in him instinctively and seek him out early in life. Some find him only in dire straits. But knowing that he lives is only a first step to finding him. Even when we find him we can lose him. Some people lose faith in God because their prayers seem to go unanswered. They don't recognize God's helping hand in giving them what was best instead of what was wanted. *The Ripple Effect - page 100*

*L*et my soul live, and it shall praise thee; and let thy judgments help me. *Psalms 119:175*

*F*ather, I have looked for you in many places and by walking many paths because I did not understand that you are right here inside me. Bless me to internalize this by faith, so that I can discern your gracious beauty in all my circumstances. I love you. And I desire to live in the light of your love always.

Affirmation: **My knowledge of God blesses me, and I will praise him as long as I live.**

September 12

Doing Service
Heals My Spirit

I began to heal. At first I started doing small things—fixing a meal for sick friends, baby-sitting for young parents who needed time to be alone together, making calls to older people who were shut in. These first small steps led to more, and then still more. I continued doing service because it required my energy and focus, and I enjoyed the love that I received in return. *The Awakening Heart - page 33*

We know that we have passed from death unto life, because we love . . . 1 John 3:14

Father, make me aware of how I can be of comfort and a resource to others whether their needs be great or small. Bless me through my service to heal from my inner hurts and to know you better as my Father. Help me feel and understand the love which you so freely give to me.

Affirmation: **I delight in the expression of Christ-like love and accept its healing powers.**

Brotherly Love Is Essential to My Life

In this world of billions of people, many lead lives of loneliness and desperation. Because of pain produced by others, some protect themselves behind walls of anger or fear, lashing out at or retreating from others. God has shown me that the precious cure for their pain lies within each soul. The cure . . . is honest and pure love. God's love. Unconditional love. It resides within each of us naturally at our beginning.
The Ripple Effect - page xvi

Let brotherly love continue . . . Remember them that are in bonds, as bound with them; and them which suffer adversity, as being yourselves . . . Hebrews 13:1, 3

Father, when the difficulties of life make me afraid or angry, remind me that the sure and divine remedy to pain is love. Help me to find love when I need it and to magnify love by sharing it freely with others. For I know that within all your children is the healing balm of love in pure expression for one another.

Affirmation: **The brotherly love I extend to all eases misery and lightens burdens.**

September 14

Many Messengers of Light
Bless Our Earth

Those who understand the message of God's love must share it with courage and confidence. People not yet sure in spiritual truth will be supported and guided by those who are sure until they come into their own understanding. We can and will see our world cleansed of all evil and blanketed with a greater glory, even the glory and love of God. But we must each believe and act in that belief. *The Ripple Effect - pages 92-93*

Blessed be God, even the Father of our Lord Jesus Christ, the Father of mercies, and the God of all comfort; Who comforteth us in all our tribulation, that we may be able to comfort them which are in any trouble, by the comfort wherewith we ourselves are comforted of God. 2 Corinthians 1:3-4

Father, bless me with confidence and love in sharing my knowledge of you with others. May what I share comfort them and strengthen them, Father, as your Spirit has comforted and strengthened me.

Affirmation: **I am confident in God's eternal love and take joy in the strength he gives me.**

September 15

God Blesses Me Through Adversity to See My Teachers

God's love is like the sun, constant and shining for us all. And just as the earth rotates around the sun, it is the natural order for us to move away for a season, and then to return closer, but always within the appropriate time. I saw now that when I had moved away, it was often for the purpose of acquiring new tools that could not have been acquired in any other way. *The Awakening Heart - page 42*

And though the Lord give you the bread of adversity, and the water of affliction, yet shall not thy teachers be removed into a corner any more, but thine eyes shall see thy teachers . . . Isaiah 30:20

Father, thank you for painful experiences which bring me face to face with what I need to learn and grow from. My afflictions drive me toward needed change, and I can see they are my greatest teachers. Thank you, father, for bringing me back when I have drifted off. I am stronger and wiser when I return to you.

Affirmation: **I am drawn to the Creator as the earth is to the sun.**

September 16

God Casts Out the Spirit of Depression

Depression is a natural home for negative energy and can be as crippling as any physical illness . . . This dilemma is real. People suffering from depression cannot escape without real effort, but they have lost the energy required to give that effort. The cycle of depression is seductive, even if we believe in God and look to him for support. So we must be watchful, and we must evaluate the little things in life that either sustain or defeat depression. *The Ripple Effect - pages 79-80*

Why art thou cast down, O my soul? and why art thou disquieted within me? hope thou in God: for I shall yet praise him, who is the health of my countenance, and my God. Psalms 42:11

Father, when I lose my will to keep going, bless me to see and find comfort in the simplest treasures in life. Help me continue finding ways to praise you while I am dismayed. Thank you for opening doors of escape from what I have believed to be inescapable, and for holding me in your loving arms of comfort.

Affirmation: **I lean on God when I am weary. He gives me comfort and rest.**

September 17

God Gives Inspiration and Guidelines for My Life

God gave me inspiration; certain things that were given to me, like mile markers. I came to learn that just before I'd collapse, I would reach that marker and say to myself, "Yes, I'm this far along. Just some more to go, Betty." And then I'd have the strength to go on some more. *The Awakening Heart - pages 104-105*

And the Lord shall guide thee continually, and satisfy thy soul in drought, and make fat thy bones: and thou shalt be like a watered garden, and like a spring of water, whose waters fail not. Isaiah 58:11

Thank you, Father, for blessing me with intuition and with feelings of satisfaction when my life unfolds as you have blessed me to know it should. These precious moments help me to continue on and to reach for greater heights that will ultimately bring me closer to you.

Affirmation: **God blesses me with insight and foreknowledge, and I know I am doing the Lord's will.**

My Heart Is
Opening to Love

As I continued the process of opening up to God and letting go, I healed more rapidly. My service to others led me to new friends, and I was blessed by their love. More important, God could reach me because of my open heart, and I began to experience again his loving presence in great abundance. *The Awakening Heart - page 35*

Beloved, if God so loved us, we ought also to love one another . . . If we love one another, God dwelleth in us, and his love is perfected in us. 1 John 4:11-12

Father, there is always room for progress in learning better how to love. Thank you for blessing me with relationships, challenges and avenues for service that bring me growth and healing. Father, I want to become Love, as you are Love. Help me to let go of old pain, resentments, and insecurities, so that I may open my heart completely and experience the joy of true closeness with you and the people around me.

Affirmation: **God dwells in me, and I give and receive his love freely.**

September 19

By Putting Faith into Action, I Inherit the Promises of God

Through my own journeys I have learned that it often seems easier not to move on; even the muck and mire in which we are stuck often seems less fearful and challenging than the unknown path ahead . . . But faith is not complacent: faith is action. You don't have faith and then wait . . . you act upon it.
The Awakening Heart - page 220

That ye be not slothful, but followers of them who through faith and patience inherit the promises.
Hebrews 6:12

Thank you, Father, for promising me blessings up ahead if I just press on through my struggles. Thank you, too, for those who stand as beacons of light, encouraging me on, bolstering my faith, reminding me to trust in your will. Bless me never to give up, but to push ahead, keeping faith alive in my heart by fearless action.

Affirmation: **I demonstrate my faith by moving forward into action.**

Spiritual Laws Govern My Spiritual Development

*L*aw exists throughout the universe. It exists, not for our torment, but for our happiness. Spiritual laws are based solely on what will lead us to greater understanding and to being Christ-like. *The Ripple Effect - page 38*

*H*appy is the man that findeth wisdom, and the man that getteth understanding. *Proverbs 3:13*

*F*ather, experience teaches me that I can not progress or be happy when I ignore your laws. Thank you for Jesus, who taught your laws and lived them perfectly. Bless me to internalize the lessons he gave and to live as he did, loving, serving and blessing others in wisdom and in charity. Increase my understanding as I use the laws that govern my growth.

Affirmation: **I obey the laws of God and increase my happiness.**

Wisdom Is Knowing
There Is More to Learn

I did not know how to express such love after my return, but I knew that I had the desire to learn. Love would come to me because I was receptive, open, and tender, and that was all that was necessary. God "knew" my heart. His love for me found no barrier, and my love for him would never end. *The Awakening Heart - page 40*

*A*nd if any man think that he knoweth any thing, he knoweth nothing yet as he ought to know. But if any man love God, the same is known of him. *1 Corinthians 8:2-3*

*F*ather, thank you for making me aware that as I remain open to growth I will expand in wisdom. Bless me with an increase of love and knowledge and a desire to do good, to become more willing to learn that which you have in store for me. And bless me, Father, to humble myself and recognize that without you I am nothing.

Affirmation: **In humility I seek the wisdom of God, my Creator, who blesses me in all things.**

September 22

The Creator Blessed the World with Life-giving Substances

I was shown that the earth, too, had a spirit life, an energy that God gave it so that it could produce life-giving substances for our benefit. Then, as its inhabitants, we lent our own energy to that energy, changing the earth's to match our own. *The Awakening Heart - pages 7-8*

The earth is full of the goodness of the Lord. Psalms 33:5

Father, thank you for creating a world that provides for all our needs. Teach us not to abuse its life-giving substances, but to preserve them for our posterity. Bless us always to show our appreciation for this earth by giving it care and enhancing it with our love. I know, Father, that being wise stewards over what you have given brings abundance and makes us ready to be stewards over greater things.

Affirmation: **My world is blessed by God and complete in his love and goodness.**

Dreams Are God-Given Imagery to Teach Us

$\mathcal{D}$reams help heal our minds and our souls. The dreamer himself is the star of most dreams, regardless of identity or gender ... Most dreams proceed in symbolic imagery, often causing difficulty in interpretation, but often leaving a sense of knowledge having been conveyed. As several events in the Bible indicate, interpreting dreams cannot be done confidently or accurately without the Spirit's guiding power. If we want to know what our dreams are telling us, we must open ourselves to the power of God. *The Ripple Effect - page 133*

$\mathcal{A}$nd they said unto him, We have dreamed a dream, and there is no interpreter of it. And Joseph said unto them, Do not interpretations belong to God? Genesis 40:8

$\mathcal{F}$ather, my mind expands to greater spiritual awareness through the visions and dreams you bless me with. Thank you for sharing your spirit in ways that still remain a mystery, but are revealed through you in time.

Affirmation: **I trust the Spirit's guiding power to reveal my dreams to me.**

September 24

God's Creations Are Perfect in Every Detail

My escorts . . . led me from the garden to a large building. As we entered it, I was impressed with its details and exquisite beauty. Buildings are perfect there . . . Every structure, every creation there is a work of art. *Embraced By The Light - page 108*

And the building of the wall of it was of jasper: and the city was pure gold, like unto clear glass. And the foundations of the wall of the city were garnished with all manner of precious stones . . . And the city had no need of the sun, neither of the moon, to shine in it: for the glory of God did lighten it, and the Lamb is the light thereof. Revelation 21:18-19, 23

Thank you, Father. All that you are, all that you create, reflects the beauty of your love and of your magnificent spirit.

Affirmation: **My God is a Master Craftsman. He designed and made me perfect.**

I Accepted Laws That Govern Me

*A*ll people as spirits in the pre-mortal world took part in the creation of the earth. We were thrilled to be part of it . . . Each spirit . . . assisted in planning the conditions on earth, including the laws of mortality which would govern us. *Embraced By The Light - page 47*

*F*or the invisible things of him from the creation of the world are clearly seen, being understood by the things that are made . . . *Romans 1:20*

*F*ather, thank you for creating me like yourself with a mind that is free to create and choose. To feel that I was present when you created the earth is a great blessing. And knowing that I understood the plan that would govern my growth gives me new perspectives on everything. When I feel disheartened or confused about the condition of my life and the world around me, help me remember that I consented to take on these many trials and that their purpose will serve you.

Affirmation: **I accept the divine wisdom behind all creation and know that I am a creator, too.**

 September 26

When I Am Ready, God Moves Me to Higher Growth

I could see that God was always moving me in the right direction; whenever I'd step off, he would gently guide me back, always putting me in a position where my faith would have to be tested. And it is in the testing of our faith that we can experience the greatest growth. *The Awakening Heart - page 130*

God is my strength and power: and he maketh my way perfect. 2 Samuel 22:33

Thank you, Father. Because you love me, you bless me with experiences that improve my faith and bring me spiritual growth beyond my comprehension. I have felt your guiding hand correcting my direction by moving me to make change.

Affirmation: **God's hand gently leads me within the circumstances of my life's challenges.**

My Closest Friends Are
Bonded to Me Eternally

I, too, had met people who had seemed familiar to me. The first time I met them I felt an instant closeness, a recognition, but hadn't known why. Now I knew that they had been sent to my path for a reason. They had always been special to me. *Embraced By The Light - page 100*

*N*ow when Job's three friends heard of all this evil that was come upon him, they came every one from his own place . . . for they had made an appointment together to come to mourn with him and to comfort him. *Job 2:11*

*F*ather, thank you for my friends who have awakened my love and blessed my life. My relationships with them are precious to me. Bless their families and their homes. And fulfill their needs, and surround them with your divine love forever.

Affirmation: **I give myself to my friends who bless my life with their eternal love.**

The Strength of My Spirit
Empowers My Thought

*B*ecause I knew that all creation begins with thoughts, I also knew that the creation of sin, and of guilt, and of despair, and of hope, and of love all start within us. All healing comes from within. All misery comes from within. *Embraced By The Light - page 71*

There is nothing from without a man, that entering into him can defile him; but the things which come out of him, those are they that defile the man . . . For from within, out of the heart of men, proceed evil thoughts . . . Mark 7:15, 21

Father, when negative thoughts seem to come from "nowhere," I will pay closer attention and search my own heart for their source. Thank you for so powerfully blessing me to have control over my life. Help me to progress beyond letting my imperfect thoughts rule my life. And bless me to lean upon your wisdom, understanding and guidance, instead.

Affirmation: **I monitor my thoughts, changing negative into positive, creating healing energies for myself and others.**

My Spiritual Strength Can Overrule My Ego

God knows beforehand what we need, but he wants us to grow by exercising our spiritual strength and constantly seeking his help in the face of opposition. The world may tell us to rely on our own egos and talents. *The Ripple Effect - page 97*

For by grace are ye saved through faith; and that not of yourselves: it is the gift of God: Not of works, lest any man should boast. *Ephesians 2:8-9*

Father, when I ask for your help, I know it is not a sign of weakness, but a demonstration of faith. Thank you for teaching me that humility shows strength and empowers the spirit. Help me give in less to my ego and more to the promptings you give through my spirit. Bless me to see that I will have success and joy in my life, not through relying upon my own strength and wits, but through spirit and faith and by your grace.

Affirmation: **My spiritual strength comes from my faith and the Spirit of God.**

September 30

God Governs Knowledge and Controls Its Power

Now I knew that there actually was a God. No longer did I believe in just a Universal Power, but now I saw the Man behind that Power. I saw a loving Being who created the universe and placed all knowledge within it. I saw that he governs this knowledge and controls its power. *Embraced By The Light - page 61*

He hath made the earth by his power, he hath established the world by his wisdom, and hath stretched out the heavens by his discretion. Jeremiah 10:12

Father, how grateful I am to know you and to feel the protection and concern only a loving Father can show. I acknowledge your supreme power and am blessed to see it in action in my life. Because of your authority and wisdom, I have confidence in your plan for my life, in your creation and in your love.

Affirmation: **I trust the gentle strength of God's power.**

October 1

My Inner Voice Speaks to My Subconscious Mind

We each have an inner voice, that deep part of our soul that recognizes pure truth. It speaks to us, confirming and teaching truth. It perfectly understands the language of the Spirit of God. It acts as our conscience, intuitively warning us from danger, both spiritual and physical. This inner voice has full access to our subconscious memories of the pre-mortal life, and this voice resonates in our beings when a hidden truth from that time is made known to us. *The Ripple Effect - page 104*

Thou gavest also thy good spirit to instruct them . . . Nehemiah 9:20

Father, I am thankful for the voice within me that witnesses and confirms your truth when I find it. Though I have forgotten my pre-mortal life with you, my inner voice speaks to me regarding the things I knew there. Thank you for blessing me with this way to access the hidden treasures of my soul.

Affirmation: **I listen to the whisperings of my inner voice. It speaks only for my good.**

October 2

The Universe Sings with Heavenly Praises of My Lord

Outside the room a glorious vista of mountains and valleys and rivers captivated me. The scene was filled with life and color and passion. I have heard the phrase "the mountains will sing at His coming." In heaven the mountains sing endlessly. Everything has energy and tone and love. Everything is alive and alert and full of joy.
The Ripple Effect - page 8

Sing, O ye heavens; for the Lord hath done it: shout, ye lower parts of the earth: break forth into singing, ye mountains, O forest, and every tree therein . . .
Isaiah 44:23

Thank you, Father, for the songs of praise and joy that fill all life in heaven with passion. How blessed we are as your children to know that this wondrous energy awaits our return for us to experience and partake in. Bless us on earth to find fulfillment here, to raise our voices in praise and song and rejoice in our creation.

Affirmation: **I think of heaven, and my spirit is full of song.**

October 3

I Open My Heart to All Who Seek God

*A*s our spiritual awareness grows, we must not condemn others who worship differently . . . After all, most of us will experience several religions in our search for truth. At each stop we may discover new truths, new opportunities. Then, if we have grown sufficiently, we may become restless again and open ourselves to yet greater truths. *The Ripple Effect - pages 115-16*

*A*nd John answered him, saying, Master, we saw one casting out devils in thy name, and he followeth not us: and we forbad him, because he followeth not us. But Jesus said, Forbid him not: for there is no man which shall do a miracle in my name, that can lightly speak evil of me. For he that is not against us is on our part. *Mark 9:38-40*

*F*ather, as I search for greater truth and understanding, help me not to condemn others for their belief. Bless me to honor my commitment to you and lead through example, not by condemnation and reproach.

Affirmation: **I respect and honor the many ways others worship the Creator.**

October 4

God Perfectly, Lovingly, Paces My Growth

We grow best when we progress at our own speed from our current beliefs to greater understanding. *The Awakening Heart - page 43*

Teach me thy statutes. I am thy servant; give me understanding, that I may know thy testimonies. Psalms 119:124-125

Father, I have much to learn in this mortal life, many trials to endure, and many joys to revel in. I am glad that I may grow toward divinity gradually, no faster than my abilities naturally compel me. This humbles me, Father, and relieves me of stress and guilt. I rejoice knowing that, as I progress in your light and truths, they are unfolded to me in greater degree.

Affirmation: **I learn and grow at the perfect rate for my own capabilities and understanding.**

My Source of Energy Is Rooted in the Power of God

We can recharge our own spirits through serving others, having faith in God, and simply opening ourselves to positive energy through positive thoughts. We control it. The source of energy is God and is always there, but we must tune him in. We must accept the power of God if we want to enjoy the effects of it in our lives. *Embraced By The Light - page 67*

That your faith should not stand in the wisdom of men, but in the power of God. 1 Corinthians 2:5

Father, your love pours into me when I have a giving heart and do service, when I show faith, or when I open myself to you. Recharge my weary spirit when I am low. And keep me grounded, not in my own imperfect wisdom and strength, but in your infinite power to save. Thank you for your life-giving love.

Affirmation: **Heavenly energy and power fill my life, and in God alone I succeed.**

October 6

To Embrace Life
Is to Embrace God

God's love and truth are the only things that permanently change hearts. Anger and insults do not. Pickets do not. Bullets and bombs do not. We are his creation and must stand in line like dominoes—close to each other, filled with love, showing by example and encouragement that the path to happiness lies not in the taking of life but in the embracing of it. *The Ripple Effect - pages 43-44*

Fulfil ye my joy, that ye be like-minded, having the same love, being of one accord, of one mind. Let nothing be done through strife or vain glory; but in lowliness of mind let each esteem the other better than themselves. Philippians 2:2-3

Thank you, Father, for my life which can be filled with joy and happiness. Help me embrace life to its fullest, to show my love for it and for you, that I may lift others by this example and draw to me in service many whose hearts and thoughts are like mine. Bless all who love you to stand together in changing the world by radiating only your love.

Affirmation: **I embrace all life because life is of God.**

October 7

God Opens His Realm
Through Visions and Dreams

Dreams have always been an important part of my expanded awareness of the spiritual realm. They can provide a gateway for communication from our loved ones in the spirit world and can also connect us with our higher self and God, affording us an opportunity to receive messages in the conscious mind. *The Awakening Heart - pages 77-78*

Hear now my words: If there be a prophet among you, I the Lord will make myself known unto him in a vision, and will speak unto him in a dream. Numbers 12:6

Father, how grateful I am to have dreams that inspire and bless me. I will remain receptive to my dreams and will ponder and pray to gain insight from their messages. But most of all, Father, I will awaken to their possibilities and learn to trust when the Spirit tells me they are from you.

Affirmation: **I accept what messages God sends through my dreams, and act upon the knowledge I receive.**

I Judge Myself More Harshly Than Does God

*I*n the midst of my pain, I felt the love of the council come over me. They watched my life with understanding and mercy. Everything about me was taken into consideration, how I was raised, the things I had been taught, the pain given me by others, the opportunities I had received or not received. And I realized that the council was not judging me. I was judging myself. Their love and mercy were absolute. Their respect for me could never be lessened. *Embraced By The Light*

- pages 112-113

*F*or if our heart condemn us; God is greater than our heart, and knoweth all things. *1 John 3:20*

*T*hank you, Father, for your wisdom and love that comfort me when I have feelings of self-condemnation. Bless me to understand that it is not my place to make judgement, even of myself. Help me to forgive myself for what I have said or done in my past when I had lesser understanding.

Affirmation: **God views my actions in loving consideration of all my circumstances.**

October 9

Placing My Heart in God's Hands, I Pray Without Ceasing

Christ encouraged his followers to pray without ceasing, meaning our hearts should always be in communication with God. Our thoughts can be prayers, too. There are times when, whatever the attitude of the body, the soul can be on its knees. As prayer warriors, those times would be continuous. *The Ripple Effect - page 95*

Pray without ceasing. 1 Thessalonians 5:17

Father, my heart, mind and soul rejoice when I feel continuously connected to you. I place my heart in your hands and ask you to mold it to serve your purpose for me. Father, you know my heart better than I do, and I trust you to guide me through all my decisions. Bless me to stay this close to you forever.

Affirmation: **My soul communicates constantly with my Creator.**

 October 10

My Reaction to a Situation Is What Matters Most

*T*rue and lasting happiness does not come from circumstance, but from within. Problems may surround us, but we have the power to transform them into teachers. It is never the situation, but how we choose to react to it, that really matters. *The Ripple Effect - page 80*

*L*et not your heart be troubled . . *John 14:1*

*F*ather, I realize that this life brings hardships and difficult situations. But I am confident that, with your help, I will respond to these times with nobility and use them for my own spiritual growth. Thank you for strengthening my character when I react to my trials with courage and honor.

*A*ffirmation: **I respond to adversities with a strong, hopeful heart.**

God's Presence Delights Me

I awakened from an afternoon nap to see lights of brilliant colors moving around me . . . I knew that I was in the presence of angels who had sung to me just before I returned to earth. With song, light, and brilliant color, they continued to express to me that whatever the struggles I was facing, I was in the right place. I was surrounded with God's love, and all was well.
The Awakening Heart - pages 35-36

The Lord thy God in the midst of thee is mighty; he will save, he will rejoice over thee with joy; he will rest in his love, he will joy over thee with singing.
Zephaniah 3:17

Father, I am grateful to feel your joyful spirit and influence when I partake of life's goodness. With your blessings I will live a righteous life and feel the presence of your angels and servants to love and aid me. Your love gives me comfort and peace.

Affirmation: **I feel God's compassionate spirit and know I am not alone.**

God Knows My Suffering and Comforts Me

God knows exactly how much suffering we can endure, and he will not allow us to suffer beyond that unless we exercise our free will and demand more. Regrettably, some people do demand more by their hardness and bitterness and refusal to love and to forgive. But God is always in control, and if his direct assistance is exactly what is needed for our spiritual growth, he gives it, willingly and lovingly. *The Ripple Effect - page 54*

Behold, we count them happy which endure. Ye have heard of the patience of Job, and have seen the end of the Lord; that the Lord is very pitiful, and of tender mercy. James 5:11

Father, at times my trials seem so great that I feel I cannot bear them alone. But I am comforted by your promise not to test me beyond my ability to endure. Thank you for being with me when I suffer and feel lost. Your spirit truly comforts me. I am blessed to have you watching over me.

Affirmation: **I rejoice that God preserves me always, in every moment of pain and suffering.**

October 13

My Spirit Will Live Beyond This Life

*I*n my fears, I had misinterpreted death, had expected something that was not so. The grave was never intended for the spirit—only for the body. *Embraced By The Light - page 43*

*T*hen shall the dust return to the earth as it was: and the spirit shall return unto God who gave it. *Ecclesiastes 12:7*

*F*ather, thank you for sending me here to experience in the flesh this life you so beautifully and carefully prepared for me. Bless me with sure understanding that I will live on after death, that I will return to your side and know the fullness of your love. Help me teach others that they, too, are your spirit children, that great joy and peace are had in viewing this life from the broader perspective of your plan.

Affirmation: **Within this robe of imperfect flesh, my glorious spirit resides.**

My Loving Actions
Illuminate My
Walk with God

Everything we do touches everybody else in some way, and . . . as we release our love to others, we each become the vessel God has chosen from the beginning. *The Ripple Effect - page xvi*

Let every one of us please his neighbor for his good to edification. *Romans 15:2*

Father, in all my relationships, help me act in ways which express loving concern. May I show kindness and an example of light and truth, even to those I do not know. Make me pure in heart, and bless me to feel joy and fulfillment in telling others of your love.

Affirmation: **I liberally give of my love and am becoming the disciple of God I am meant to be.**

October 15

Because I Forgive, I Am Forgiven

What I give out is what I receive. If I want forgiveness, I have to give forgiveness. *Embraced By The Light - page 116*

Judge not, and ye shall not be judged: condemn not, and ye shall not be condemned: forgive, and ye shall be forgiven. Luke 6:37

Father, help me not to condemn what I do not understand in others, and help me to forgive in them that which I see in myself. Bless me with the ability to see beyond what I might deem a "sin" and to trust that your guiding hand is leading others to find the truth needed for their lives. Thank you, Father, for teaching me to leave judgement to you and your perfect wisdom.

Affirmation: **I cleanse myself from all unrighteousness, and there is forgiveness in my heart.**

Our Omnipotent God Is Father of All

"God" is a way to express the Ultimate Source, the Omnipotence, but the God I met was more like a father, someone personal and loving, not just an authority figure. *The Awakening Heart - page 46*

One God and Father of all, who is above all, and through all, and in you all. *Ephesians 4:6*

Thank you, Father, for the grace with which you use your ever abundant power. And thank you for acknowledging me as your child. I feel your love more personally when I call you "Father." I see in myself the potential to become more like you. I love you, Father.

Affirmation: **The Ultimate Source in my life is my personal and loving Father.**

Jesus Is My Brother, Savior, and Friend

I felt his enormous spirit and knew that I had always been a part of him, that in reality I had never been away from him . . . There was no questioning who he was. I knew that he was my Savior, and friend, and God. He was Jesus Christ, who had always loved me, even when I thought he hated me. He was life itself, love itself, and his love gave me a fullness of joy, even to overflowing. I knew that I had known him from the beginning, from long before my earth life, because my spirit remembered him. *Embraced By The Light - pages 41-42*

Greater love hath no man than this, that a man lay down his life for his friends. Ye are my friends . . . Henceforth I call you not servants . . . but I have called you friends; for all things that I have heard of my Father I have made known unto you. John 15:13-15

Father, blessed be the name of my brother, Jesus Christ. As he evolved to become one with you, he fulfilled his mission, which was to set an example for us to follow.

Affirmation: **Because he gave his life for me, I know no greater friend than Jesus.**

October 18

God Reveals Much Through
Inner Promptings

Being a wise and impartial God, he blesses all who reach out to him, granting them knowledge and faith. All who are open to truth and are willing to live by it once they receive it, will receive more—by visions or visitations or, more likely, by quiet prompting and insights. *The Ripple Effect - page 2*

Call unto me, and I will answer thee, and show thee great and mighty things, which thou knowest not.
Jeremiah 33:3

Thank you, Father, for your enthusiasm to share with us all that is great and wonderful in heaven. I honor what you desire for me in life and will do humbly whatever you ask of me, that your purpose and your will be fulfilled in me. Help me to live more honestly by the truths you have revealed to me, and make me worthy and responsible for greater teachings. Bless me with the capacity to receive your truth by whatever means you deliver it.

Affirmation: **I am open to God's promptings and insights. I am ready to learn greater truths.**

October 19

The Energy of My Soul Is Love

We were conceived in love spiritually, and love is the center of our beings. It is the energy of our souls, the spark of our divine nature. Being made of love, we cleave to it and seek it in all that we do. When we do not have it, or when we have lost it, we grieve. Its presence or absence colors our every action. It is life. It is happiness. It is salvation itself. *The Ripple Effect - page 145*

God is love; and he that dwelleth in love dwelleth in God, and God in him. 1 John 4:16

Thank you, Father, for the empowering influence of your Spirit. You are love and the energy of my soul. Bless me to draw from your love the strength to endure and complete my purpose in life. Teach me to use the energy of your love to express goodness and to bless others who are seeking it still.

Affirmation: **My soul's energy is God's love.**

Growing Within Me Is God's Eternal Truth

Sometimes in the course of life we make wrong choices, and in the wisdom of God, he may arrange the circumstances to let us try again. His love is unconditional. This is the greatest, most prevalent truth in existence. We did not come to earth to earn our way back to him. We came to experience and develop that which had existed in us through the "eternities." *The Ripple Effect - page 206*

Though our outward man perish, yet the inward man is renewed day by day. For our light affliction, which is but for a moment, worketh for us a far more exceeding and eternal weight of glory . . . 2 Corinthians 4:16-17

Father, through eternities past you led me step by step to learn your truths and know your will. Bring me now, through experience and insight, to new understanding and greater growth. Renew my spirit in wisdom to learn from my trials and mistakes. Make me ever grateful for eternal growth in becoming more like you.

Affirmation: **I nourish God's truth within me, and my spirit is growing strong.**

October 21

Gratitude Is Important to Opening My Heart

We must learn to be grateful for whatever trials and gifts our Father gives us in the journey. There is magic in gratitude. It frees us from worry and competition in life. It opens our hearts and hands to genuine love, ironically allowing our hearts and hands to be filled again. *The Ripple Effect - page 30*

Let us offer the sacrifice of praise to God continually, that is, the fruit of our lips giving thanks to his name.
Hebrews 13:15

Father, help me pause during my day to think on your many blessings and to lift a prayer of thanksgiving to you. Bless me to discern even in adversity your gifts which refine and strengthen me. Help me use every new-found strength, every blessing you send, to serve and bless others in need. By this, Father, I pray I show my thankfulness.

Affirmation: **I am grateful for every facet of my life, and for all that it reflects.**

I Can Draw Upon the Powers of Heaven

God wants us to become as he is, and . . . has invested us with godlike qualities . . . I understood that he wants us to draw on the powers of heaven, and that by believing that we are capable of doing so, we can.
Embraced By The Light - page 61

And Stephen, full of faith and power, did great wonders and miracles among the people. Acts 6:8

Father, because you are my Heavenly Father and have blessed me with your godlike qualities, the powers of heaven are available to me. Thank you for using your knowledge and wisdom to teach me to use my powers wisely. Bless me to receive added spiritual power according to your perfect understanding when I have grown to receive more.

Affirmation: **I draw upon the powers of heaven and am capable of doing great things.**

October 23

My Spirit Delights to Witness God in All Things

The search for God's presence in my life was more important now than ever before. I was compelled first to find him in everything that surrounded me, then to seek his presence within me. When I began to see him unexpectedly, everywhere, in everyone and everything, my soul delighted, and I felt as a child would feel, seeing everything for the first time and from a clearer perspective. *The Awakening Heart - page 37*

Seek the Lord and his strength, seek his face continually. *1 Chronicles 16:11*

Thank you, Father, when I look for you, I always find you . . . in a smile, a hug, in incidental change of circumstances or events, in an evening rain. To know that you are always with me, always ready to help, always ready to inspire gives me tremendous comfort and joy. Help me share these daily revelations with the people in my life, and bless me to live in such a way that others clearly see your presence in me.

Affirmation: **My soul thrills to the presence of God in everything.**

I Pray For the Gift of Self-Forgiveness

Forgiveness of self is where all forgiveness starts. If I am unable to forgive myself, it is impossible for me to truly forgive others. And I must forgive others. *Embraced By The Light - page 116*

But if ye do not forgive, neither will your Father which is in heaven forgive your trespasses. *Mark 11:26*

Father, when I do wrong, forgiving my self is often hard to do. Comfort my heart by reminding me that I am still learning and growing in perfection. Let me not get lost in guilt or in fear that I displease you. Thank you for showing me how my mistakes teach me, how they give me experience, understanding and finally wisdom.

Affirmation: **Mistakes are my beloved teachers that bring me to the Fathers will.**

Nothing in Life Is Random or Accidental

There are far fewer accidents here than we imagine, especially in things that affect us eternally. The hand of God and the path we chose before we came here guide many of our decisions and even many of the seemingly random experiences we have . . . Even experiences such as divorce, sudden unemployment, or being a victim of violence may ultimately give us knowledge and contribute to our spiritual development.
Embraced By The Light - pages 68-69

Affliction cometh not forth of the dust, neither doth trouble spring out of the ground . . . Job 5:6

Father, thank you for walking beside me during times of sorrow in my life. I know that you permit me to sow and reap those things which ultimately serve to bless me with wisdom and knowledge. Teach me to learn from my problems and then to take my understanding further in blessing me to use all things for your glory.

Affirmation: **Every experience brings positive purpose and meaning to my life.**

I Have Lived in
God's Everlasting Love Forever

*E*ach morning I awoke, my thoughts were the same. I was homesick for a place that did not exist here on earth, a place that my heart longed for . . . I so missed the warmth of God's eternal, unconditional love. *The Awakening Heart - pages 23-24*

*L*ord, thou hast been our dwelling place in all generations. Before the mountains were brought forth, or ever thou hadst formed the earth and the world, even from everlasting to everlasting, thou art God. *Psalms 90:1-2*

Father, though I work diligently to be a proper steward of this earthly home, I know my true home is with you on high. I have learned through your grace and guiding influence that in the light of your love is the only place I long to be.

Affirmation: **The dwelling place of my soul is in the presence of my Eternal Father.**

By Grace I Am
Quickened with Jesus to
Have Eternal Life

$\mathcal{A}$s I saw his arms open to receive me I went to him and received his complete embrace . . . And I knew that I was worthy to be with him, to embrace him. I knew that he was aware of all my sins and faults, but that they didn't matter right now. He just wanted to hold me and share his love with me, and I wanted to share mine with him.
Embraced By The Light - pages 41-42

$\mathcal{B}$ut God, who is rich in mercy, for his great love wherewith he loved us, Even when we were dead in sins, hath quickened us together with Christ, (by grace ye are saved;) And hath raised us up together, and made us sit together in heavenly places in Christ Jesus . . . Ephesians 2:4-6

$\mathcal{T}$hank you, Father, for by your grace and understanding, I have your forgiveness and love and a place with my Saviour, Jesus Christ. Increase my understanding that we truly have been "raised up" together and will return again to you.

$\mathcal{A}$ffirmation: **I am worthy of Jesus' embrace.**

October 28

My Prayers Delight the Heavenly Hosts

I saw angels rushing to answer the prayers. They were organized to give as much help as possible. As they worked within this organization, they literally flew from person to person, from prayer to prayer, and were filled with love and joy by their work. They delighted to help us and were especially joyful when somebody prayed with enough intensity and faith to be answered immediately. *Embraced By The Light - pages 103-04*

*A*nd when we cried unto the Lord, he heard our voice, and sent an angel . . . *Numbers 20:16*

*F*ather, thank you for giving me a way to communicate directly with you. While I know the angels are organized to guard and protect me, I also know they do it at the command of your voice. Bless me not to take prayer lightly, but to pray with earnest desire and gratitude.

Affirmation: **I pray in faith, and angels, guided by God's loving will, respond to my every prayer.**

October 29

Warring Angels Protect in Times of Need

There are other types of angels, including a type called "Warring Angels." It was shown to me that their purpose is to do battle for us against Satan and his angels. Although we each have protecting, or guardian, spirits to assist us, there are times when the Warring Angels are necessary to protect us, and I understood that they are available to us through prayer. *Embraced By The Light - page 90*

Bless the Lord, ye his angels, that excel in strength, that do his commandments, hearkening unto the voice of his word. Psalms 103:20

Father, thank you for protecting me while I grow more competent in my faith. And thank you for the strength of angels who aid me when I lose my light and have nothing more to give. Bless me to be most grateful for their swift response when I need them to protect the ones I love.

Affirmation: **The power and protection of God's Warring Angels are mine through prayer.**

Discernment Helps Me in My Prayers

Sometimes we need to pray for discernment to know what to pray for. If we pray for a gift that continues to elude us, we may be missing the lesson we are supposed to learn. Perhaps we are to work more on our own to earn the gift, or perhaps we are to learn to live without the gift, or possibly we are to continue praying for it, which stretches faith and teaches patience. *The Ripple Effect - page 102*

Ye ask, and receive not, because ye ask amiss . . .
James 4:3

Father, when I pray, bless me to come humbly before you and invite your Spirit to be with me and to guide my thoughts and words. Let me discern my spirit's desires so that I pray straight from my heart. Bless me also to exercise faith in understanding your desires for me. Give me strength to accept your answers as they come and to learn by them.

Affirmation: **I pray, discerning my heart's desire and accepting the purity of God's will.**

My Soul Searches All Things Taught of God

We are born to this earth with our soul, the pure part of us we bring to earth from the spirit world. As we develop, we lose some contact with that spiritual part, our divine self, in a process of forgetting that is necessary for our development. To feel whole again, each of us can and must reconnect with our spiritual self . . . *The Awakening Heart - page 215*

But God hath revealed them unto us by his Spirit: for the Spirit searcheth all things, yea, the deep things of God. For what man knoweth the things of a man, save the spirit of man which is in him? even so the things of God knoweth no man, but the Spirit of God. 1 Corinthians 2:10-11

Father, though I have forgotten our personal times together, my soul is still connected with you and aware of the love we have always shared. I ask you, Father, to reveal unto me the deeper desires of your heart for me that I may completely reconnect with you.

Affirmation: **I am aware of my divinity and my soul is connected with God.**

November 1

I Prosper When I Am True to Laws that Govern Me

I understood that by living true to the laws that govern us we will be further blessed and will receive still greater knowledge. But I also understood that breaking these laws, "sinning," will weaken and possibly destroy all that we have achieved up to that time. There is a cause and effect relationship to sin. We create many of our own punishments through the actions we commit. *Embraced By The Light - pages 55-56*

*A*nd keep the charge of the Lord thy God, to walk in his ways, to keep his statutes, and his commandments . . . that thou mayest prosper in all that thou doest . . . *1 Kings 2:3*

*F*ather, forgive me when my actions do not align with love and I break your law. Help me respond to situations with wisdom in using your laws, which opens the door to your blessings and to my greater understanding and development. Bless me to move beyond the "sin," to let go of self-punishment so that I may make life better for me and those I love.

Affirmation: **I follow God's laws to live a full and prosperous life.**

November 2

The Quality of My Life Is Created by Me

My rebirth into this world had at first brought me fear of this distant place, far from my original home; now I began to see its beauty. I awoke each morning to feelings of expectation, excited that God had given me another day to experience life. *The Awakening Heart - page 37*

This is the day which the Lord hath made; we will rejoice and be glad in it. Psalms 118:24

Father, thank you for blessing me with another day in which to create and to experience joy. Draw me near to you daily that I may enjoy continuous beauty and expectations of fuller life with you. You are my joy, my life, my goal.

Affirmation: **I relish the new awakening each day brings, and am closer to achieving my goals.**

I Release All Bitterness and Strife to God

We must forgive until always and forever. Christ gives us this law, not for our punishment or difficulty, but for our peace and happiness. Without a forgiving heart, we will never open ourselves to the gift of being healed. We cannot do it, because the purest gift of his love is the ability to love completely, without reservation, without hatred, without hesitation. Love is the energy that heals even the deepest pain. *The Ripple Effect - page 57*

Let all bitterness, and wrath, and anger, and clamor, and evil speaking, be put away from you, with all malice: And be ye kind one to another, tenderhearted, forgiving one another, even as God for Christ's sake hath forgiven you. Ephesians 4:31-32

Father, thank you for lessons that teach me what I need to stay healthy and happy. I am learning that I must forgive and release the bitterness, anger and strife which injure my spirit and cause disease. Only then am I receptive to your love and can begin to heal.

Affirmation: **I forgive all pain, and my soul is well and whole.**

Eternal Connections
Unite Us on Earth

I had learned during my experience that my children were previously developed spiritual beings like myself. We were friends before this earth life, and we wanted to remain together for this life's lessons and experiences. We had bonded as soul friends there and chose to come here as a family . . .
The Awakening Heart - page 18

*N*ow therefore when I come to thy servant my father, and the lad be not with us; seeing that his life is bound up in the lad's life . . . thy servants shall bring down the gray hairs of . . . our father with sorrow . . .
Genesis 44:30-31

*F*ather, how wondrous to know that my family members and friends knew me before this life. I regard them more preciously and want to interact with them from the loving perspective of our eternal souls. Bless me with kindness and wisdom in word and deed so that I may help them reach their highest purpose in life.

Affirmation: **I fulfill my heavenly promises to family and friends.**

November 5

The Fruit of the Spirit
Is Love

*A*s long as we have life here, we are learning, our spirits are growing, and we are coming closer to the divine, even by the things we suffer. We may not always know what to do in our lives, we may be troubled and in pain, but be assured, as long as we are here, we are growing. We are only here for divine purposes, and the greatest divine purpose of all is to love. *The Ripple Effect - page 16*

If we live in the Spirit, let us also walk in the Spirit . . . the fruit of the Spirit is love . . . Galatians 5:22, 25

Father, there are times when I am lost, when confusion and doubt distort my view, and I feel troubled and alone. Help me remember, even in my darkest moments, that Jesus descended beneath all things to bring reconciliation, to open the way for me to return to your comforting arms and love.

Affirmation: **All things are designed for my growth and for returning me to Heavenly Father's love.**

Love's Sustaining Energy
Upholds My Soul

God began to place in my life people who carried spiritual energy that could sustain me along the way. I had been shown during my experience that we draw energy from each other—some people we receive energy from and some draw energy from us—in a constant exchange. *The Awakening Heart - page 102*

Behold, God is mine helper: the Lord is with them that uphold my soul. Psalms 54:4

Thank you, Father, for placing many souls in my life who add the power of their love to mine. Their loving strength upholds my spirit and lifts me when my own loving energy weakens. Bless me to sense when someone needs my greater love. Then bless me to give it willingly, without shame or fear.

Affirmation: **Through all his creation, both in heaven and on earth, God sustains me by his love.**

November 7

My Creator Is
My Greatest Counselor

*I*n some cases, we may need help identifying our fears, and wise counsel is valuable. But the greatest Counselor of all is our Creator, and we can bring ourselves before him at any time, in any moment, to seek his help. When we do, we open ourselves instantly to the powers of heaven and to the fullness of life, complete with the growth and happiness our Heavenly Father intended for us from the beginning. *The Ripple Effect - page 80*

Fear thou not; for I am with thee: be not dismayed; for I am thy God: I will strengthen thee; yea, I will help thee; yea, I will uphold thee . . . Isaiah 41:10

Father, I am learning that fear is a great hindrance to my spirit, and that to grow in spirit, I must lose my fears. You are my greatest helper in this, so please bless me, Father, with gentle reminders to come to you in prayer for your guidance. For you delight in helping me to know myself and in giving me peace through understanding. All I need is to humble myself before you and ask.

Affirmation: **I counsel daily with God and receive his full support and comforting peace.**

November 8

Any Step That Brings Me Closer to God Is Good

$\mathcal{N}$o one church can fulfill everybody's needs at every level; there is no "perfect" religion for all of us here. I had been shown that, because we are at various levels of spirituality, any step closer to God is good, so we should never criticize any church or faith where people are seeking God. *The Awakening Heart - page 41*

The heavens declare the glory of God; and the firmament sheweth his handywork. Day unto day uttereth speech, and night unto night sheweth knowledge. There is no speech nor language, where their voice is not heard. Their line is gone out through all the earth, and their words to the end of the world. In them hath he set a tabernacle for the sun . . . Psalms 19:1-4

Father, as you draw me nearer to you, hold my tongue from criticizing others for the ways in which you are able to draw them nearer to you. Help me embrace all who sincerely seek you, and encourage those who need my help.

Affirmation: **I grow closer to God and let old concepts and beliefs fade.**

Gratitude Is a Powerful Cure for Negativity

Gratitude . . . helps ward off negativity. Being grateful for the good things in life invites their continued influence. But remaining positive in difficult times requires a maturity that comes from experience. *The Ripple Effect - page 76*

We are troubled on every side, yet not distressed; we are perplexed, but not in despair . . . 2 Corinthians 4:8

Father, gratitude fills my heart not only for my moments of joy, but for those times I suffer pain. In expressing my thanks, I come to recognize your wisdom in all things. In acknowledging your hand in my life, I feel the influence of the Spirit abiding with me. How sweet is the comfort of your perfect plan.

Affirmation: **I am grateful to God for my life, and his blessings flow freely to me.**

My Faith Matures Through Daily Use

We are to live by faith, not by sight. Sight is involved with the cognitive, the analytical mind. It rationalizes and justifies. Faith is governed by the spirit. The spirit is emotional, accepting, and internalizes. And, as with every other attribute, the way to gain faith is to practice the use of it. If we learn to use what we have, we will receive more. This is a spiritual law. *Embraced By The Light - page 65*

Even so faith, if it hath not works, is dead, being alone. James 2:17

Thank you, Father, for blessing me with this walk of faith which is my life. I know you will guide me to the right paths and never fail me. Bless me to show my faith by exercising what I know of your truths. Help me also to strengthen my beliefs by trusting your Spirit to direct me in their use.

Affirmation: **My faith is strengthened daily by what I do.**

God Sees
All Things Perfectly

God not only hears our prayers, but he knows our needs well before we do . . . God has a vantage point we can never perceive. He sees into our eternal pasts and futures and knows our eternal needs. In his great love he answers prayers according to this eternal and omniscient perspective. He answers all prayers perfectly. *Embraced By The Light - page 106*

If any of you lack wisdom, let him ask of God, that giveth to all men liberally, and upbraideth not; and it shall be given him. But let him ask in faith, nothing wavering. For he that wavereth is like a wave of the sea driven with the wind and tossed. Every good gift and every perfect gift is from above, and cometh down from the Father of lights . . . James 1:5-6,17

Father, my sight is limited, but you see all things perfectly—my past, present and future. I am grateful that you do and that I can call upon you for guidance any time. Bless me always to do so and to act upon your answers when they come. Thank you, Father.

Affirmation: **My prayers invite God's omniscient perspective.**

November 12

The Light of Jesus
Heals and Expands My Soul

The rays of light surrounding Jesus were filled with knowledge and love. Just standing in his presence and absorbing it gave me the ability to expand the love and knowledge within. My spiritual body filled to almost bursting with his divine love and understanding. *The Awakening Heart - page 16*

For thou wilt light my candle: the Lord my God will enlighten my darkness. *Psalms 18:28*

Father, I yearn to be filled with understanding and to have a greater capacity to love. Let me feel the influence of your Son's perfect light. And bless me with a discerning heart and a sensitive spirit that I may receive the knowledge and love which prevails when I follow Jesus.

Affirmation: **I walk in the glorious light of Jesus Christ, and expand in knowledge and love.**

In My Innermost Sacred Place I Welcome God

Going to a quiet, secluded place can remove us from the cares and pressures of life and open our hearts and minds to divine promptings. A quiet place can be in nature or in an empty room. Jesus told his followers to pray in their closets, meaning that they should pray in private and from the innermost part of their hearts. *The Ripple Effect - page 105*

But thou, when thou prayest, enter into thy closet, and when thou hast shut thy door, pray to thy Father which is in secret; and thy Father which seeth in secret shall reward thee openly. *Matthew 6:6*

Father, when my heart is tender and loving, I am eager to welcome you in. Forgive me for those times when I am not so eager, when I attempt to hide what is not right within me. Bless me to know that you never pull away . . . even when I am hiding . . . but that you patiently wait for me to see that any distance between us is created by me.

Affirmation: **The Lord is present, and my heart rejoices in him.**

I Am Responsible for My Choices

By granting us free will, as I had been shown, God gave us the privilege to express ourselves and to accept the responsibility of choice—or the burden of choice, depending upon what our motivations were.
The Awakening Heart - page 38

Thou hast clothed me with skin and flesh, and . . . hast granted me life and favour, and thy visitation hath preserved my spirit. Job 10:11-12

Father, how marvelous is this gift of choice you have given me. I will respect and honor it by seeking to choose righteously. Through wise choices I prove myself worthy of the gift; through poor, I learn by paying a price. Enlighten me, Father, in all my choosing, for I depend upon your wisdom and insight. Bless me to prove myself worthy and capable in using this and all gifts you have given to me.

Affirmation: **I choose responsibily and respect all opportunities to advance in my understanding of God .**

November 15

Heavenly Father's Pleasure
Is to Bless Me

God already knows that our wisdom is often "insufficient for the day," but before violating our personal agency, he will often wait to help until we ask him to. If we recognize him as our father and ourselves as his children, our prayers will occur naturally. We will understand that we don't need to change his mind, we only need to open ourselves to the blessings he already wishes to give us. *The Ripple Effect - page 96*

Fear not, little flock; for it is your Father's good pleasure to give you the kingdom. Luke 12:32

Father, I delight in the warmth of your paternal love, and the blessings you freely give me. You have blessed me to express myself as I choose, but let me feel the relationship between us that draws me to you as your child. Let me remember that communication with you is my opportunity to learn your will, and not attempt to impose mine upon you. Thank you for bringing me to seek your counsel.

Affirmation: **I invite the will of God into my life, and God leads me to his kingdom of love.**

 *November 16*

Heavenly Father Is the
Giver of All Gifts

A deliberate flaw is left in everything that Native Americans make. They leave them as reminders that nothing created by man can be perfect, because only the Creator is perfect. On my [native] dress is a little hand-stitched patch . . . when I start feeling a little too much pride in my accomplishments, I . . . find the stitches that remind me that I am nothing without God, and only he is perfect. *The Awakening Heart - page 145*

*A*nd when thy herds and thy flocks multiply, and thy silver and thy gold is multiplied, and all that thou hast is multiplied; Then thine heart be lifted up, and thou forget the Lord thy God, which brought thee forth . . . from the house of bondage . . . *Deuteronomy 8:13-14*

*T*hank you, Father, for little reminders that I am imperfect, that no success comes independent of you. Take away any spirit of pride that I may have in me that seeks to claim glory for what comes by your hand.

Affirmation: **I acknowledge the Father as Creator of all things.**

November 17

My Ultimate Purpose
Is to Love Others

*A*ll who would be led into our paths would lead us to our ultimate achievement. We were to be tested under challenging conditions to see how we would live the most important commandment of all—to love one another. We are all collectively bonded to each other while on earth, united in this one supreme purpose—to learn to love one another. *The Ripple Effect - pages 96-97*

*O*we no man any thing, but to love one another: for he that loveth another hath fulfilled the law. *Romans 13:8*

*F*ather, since my highest goal is to become more like you, I will show love toward everyone you send to my life. Some are easy to love, others are not, but it is loving those who are difficult or who reject my love that brings the greater growth to my character and spirit. Bless me to follow your will in all my loving actions. And help me fulfill your commandment to love all your children, regardless of circumstance.

Affirmation: **I observe with gladness God's commandment to love everyone unconditionally.**

November 18

Jesus Taught That We Share a Common Father

*H*e was the Son of God . . . chosen from before the creation of the world to be our Savior . . . I understood, to my surprise, that Jesus was a separate being from God, with his own divine purpose, and I knew that God was our mutual Father. *Embraced By The Light - pages 44, 47*

*J*esus saith unto her, Touch me not; for I am not yet ascended to my Father: but go to my brethren, and say unto them, I ascend unto my Father, and your Father; and to my God, and your God. *John 20:17*

*F*ather, you and Jesus and I are one family. We are one in heart, mind and soul. Though separated, we serve in unison, sharing one cause, one purpose, one goal. Thank you for creating me in your likeness and with your own attributes. Bless me to carry out my part in your plan, to follow my Brother Jesus in aligning my life with your divine will.

Affirmation: **I am one with my Heavenly Father and with Jesus Christ.**

November 19

The Unseen World
Vibrates with Life and Energy

To understand the power of the "unseen world" we should understand what it is composed of. Everything in the universe is made of energy, including our bodies and spirits. All that exists, materially and spiritually, contains energies which vibrate at various speeds. *The Ripple Effect - page 72*

For by him were all things created, that are in heaven, and that are in earth, visible and invisible, whether they be thrones, or dominions, or principalities, or powers: all things were created by him . . . Colossians 1:16

Father, as I come to understand the miracle of creation and the glory of your hand in all that is, bless me to appreciate both the seen and unseen worlds. You are the source of all light, power and energy in the universe. My own body and spirit have their life in you. Bless me to send out through my thoughts and desires, ripples of goodness and love which will replicate and grow to bless the world.

Affirmation: **I recognize the energy that exists in all things, and acknowledge God's wisdom in his creation.**

My Creator's Love
Empowers Me

*H*ow empowering it is to know that we are so blessed, so directed by our Creator, to know that even in our weaknesses he never gives up on us. He encourages us in unending and marvelous ways to find and use our natural strengths for higher purposes, for a higher plan. *The Ripple Effect - page 143*

*F*or my strength is made perfect in weakness. Most gladly therefore will I rather glory in my infirmities, that the power of Christ may rest upon me. *2 Corinthians 12:9*

*F*ather, I am weak, but your love strengthens me. Keep me near you always. And bless me to see my weakness without harsh judgement, so that I can be empowered by focusing on my strengths. Teach me to use the weaknesses I cannot overcome, to serve you in some small way.

Affirmation: **My weaknesses are natural strengths made perfect by God's higher plan.**

What I Give
Returns to Bless Me

$\mathcal{I}$ once heard that "you find love when you give it away." That made sense to me because that was exactly what happened to me in my embrace with the Lord. He gave me love, and I returned it, not knowing that I had love to give. *The Awakening Heart - page 40*

Lord, thou knowest all things; thou knowest that I love thee . . . John 21:17

Father, you are love because you give love unconditionally. Help me to emulate you and Jesus by growing in the love I share. Bless me to give it more freely within wisdom and honor and respect. Let me live within the laws that govern giving and receiving it, so I will receive the fullness of your blessings. Thank you, Father, for the purity of love that Jesus gained from you.

Affirmation: **The love I give returns to bless me many times over.**

November 22

Angels Walk
Among Us on Earth

Sometimes God foresees circumstances in our lives that will need to be changed for our good, and he intervenes in one way or another. When he does, however, he always honors our freedom and agency to do whatever we choose. To intervene, he may place certain persons into our lives to guide or persuade us in a new direction. Or he may give us meaningful dreams or place influential thoughts into our heads. He may send divine beings to inform us or protect us. *The Ripple Effect - pages 125-126*

Be not forgetful to entertain strangers: for thereby some have entertained angels unawares. Hebrews 13:2

Father, thank you for the times you have sent a perfect stranger to assist me in my need. These strangers are Earth Angels to me; people who are loving and willing to do service unselfishly. Let me, in turn, step forward to help when you open my eyes to someone's need.

Affirmation: **God honors me with angels of flesh who are generous and kind to all people.**

Sharing My Light
Casts Out Darkness

If each of us shares our light, soon all dark corners will be reached, and we will begin the healing of the world by chasing out darkness. We, too, will begin the healing of our own souls. *The Ripple Effect - page xvi*

The path of the just is as the shining light, that shineth more and more unto the perfect day. Proverbs 4:18

Father, no greater love, truth or wisdom shines forth like yours and that of your Son Jesus. I seek to become refined and as you are: a glorious shining example of that which is perfect. May my attempts to be just and upright with others encourage them to also follow the example of our Lord.

Affirmation: **I share my knowledge of God gladly by my example.**

The Glory Given Jesus by the Father Is Everlasting

*H*e was Jesus, my Lord and Savior . . . Although this light shone brightly around him, I saw that he was the light and it came from within him . . . Prisms of intense light spiraled, pulsated, and moved with each miniscule change in his thoughts or desires. His eyes, though liquid with his love, somehow danced like fire, flickering with energy and life when he needed to express to me his most sincere and earnest wishes for me. *The Awakening Heart - page 15*

The sun shall be no more thy light by day; neither for brightness shall the moon give light unto thee: but the Lord shall be unto thee an everlasting light, and thy God thy glory. Isaiah 60:19

Father, how grateful I am for the life and atonement of your son, my Friend and Brother Jesus Christ. Simply thinking of his countenance brings me renewed hope, love and peace. His love upholds me in times of disappointment, and inspires me to follow him in his path of perfect knowledge and truth.

Affirmation: **I follow unceasingly my Lord Jesus, whose path is as clear and bright as the sun.**

November 25

The Presence Of Love Expands My Spirit

*B*efore my return, I noticed that my spirit also emanated an abundance of light—light that was full to overflowing with love! It was [Jesus'] presence of love that I had absorbed, and it expanded me . . . Like attracts like. Just as fear is contagious, so is love. My desire to love and be loved was evident in my countenance. *The Awakening Heart - page 40*

*A*nd the grace of our Lord was exceeding abundant with faith and love which is in Christ Jesus. *1 Timothy 1:14*

*F*ather, bless me to walk in paths you would choose and to seek holy, pure and noble things in life. May I know the glory of unconditional love, not only as I receive it from you, but as I give it to others.

Affirmation: **I attract and embrace the splendor of love energy.**

Life Force from God Energizes All That Is Created

*I*n every moment of our existence we tap into the energies surrounding us. We acquire the energy of plants as we eat them, smell them, feel them, wear them. We acquire the energy of animals in the same ways. We exchange energy with other individuals as we interact with them, touch them, hear them, look at them, even by reading their words. *The Ripple Effect - page 73*

*I*t is good and comely for one to eat and to drink, and to enjoy the good of all his labour that he taketh under the sun all the days of his life, which God giveth him: for it is his portion. *Ecclesiastes 5:18*

*F*ather, thank you for the many forms of life you have created. Plants and trees produce food and medicine and blanket the earth with their wondrous beauty and fragrance. You also blessed us with animals and birds; some to clothe our bodies and cover our feet, some as food, and others as loving companions whose spiritual energy and intelligence is seen in their eyes and felt through their spirits.

Affirmation: **My Creator's vital energy flows to me from all his creation.**

November 27

Belief in God Brings
Joy and Life to My Soul

As we allow ourselves to believe in God and to accept his love, a quiet joy will rekindle our souls, a joy we will instantly want to share with others. And as we share it lovingly, that spark of joyful heaven will begin to swell within us, filling our entire souls.
The Ripple Effect - page 13

Rejoice ye in that day, and leap for joy: for, behold, your reward is great in heaven . . . Luke 6:23

Father, I believe in you and freely accept your love. Lasting joy fills my soul at thoughts of returning to my home with you in heaven. Bless me to share my excitement with others and to express my knowledge of you, that I may awaken in them also a sweet longing for your loving embrace.

Affirmation: **My soul rejoices in knowing God, my own dear Heavenly Father.**

The Duality of Life Brings Eventual Balance

During my experience, I learned that there are two parts to every person. They can be described in various ways: male and female, intellectual and emotional, protective and nurturing, right brain and left brain. Often . . . we go through life being one way or the other, but we can learn to balance both parts . . . Being off balance, too far one way or the other . . . keeps the spirit away from where it needs to be to achieve its greatest growth.
The Awakening Heart - pages 129-130

The very God of peace sanctify you wholly . . . your whole spirit and soul and body . . . 1 Thessalonians 5:23

Father, show me how to be balanced in spirit and flesh. Bless me to recognize all the qualities of my being and then to bring them forward in ways which produce harmony and strength. Thank you for every attribute you have created in me.

Affirmation: **I am sensitive to all that I am, and I equalize my life in all its wondrous parts. I am whole.**

God Helps Me Keep
Commitments Made in Heaven

*A*ll of us have made commitments in the spirit world to help each other. But we are slow to keep our covenants made so long ago. So the Lord sends angels to prompt us, to help us be true to these obligations. He won't force us, but he can prompt us. We don't know who these beings are—they appear like anybody else—but they are with us more often than we know. *Embraced By The Light - page 101*

*B*ehold, I send an Angel before thee, to keep thee in the way, and to bring thee into the place which I have prepared. *Exodus 23:20*

*F*ather, you never falter in keeping your word. Teach me to do likewise so that when I return to you, I will stand in a place of honor for keeping the covenants I made in heaven. Thank you for whispering to my spirit when I stray off course, and for redirecting my path back toward you.

Affirmation: **God sends angels to prompt and inspire me to continue in his will.**

Dreams Reveal My Life's Hidden Facets

$\mathcal{D}$reams and visions are often brief partings of the veil which allow our souls a peek into heaven. By them we discover there is more to life than what our everyday senses tell us. Dreams and visions help us to see our actions in all their facets: in the beauty of harmony and abundance, or in the nightmarish details of things we ought to change within ourselves or in our circumstances.
The Ripple Effect - page 143

$\mathcal{B}$ut there is a God in heaven that revealeth secrets, and maketh known . . . what shall be . . . Thy dream, and the visions of thy head upon thy bed, are these . . .
Daniel 2:28

$\mathcal{F}$ather, make me wise in observing the images and impressions that come as guidance from you in dreams and visions. Help me to grasp the potential realities revealed, so that I will make changes in my life or acknowledge my spiritual path and its importance to you.

Affirmation: **I am awakened to dreams and visions that direct my journey toward love.**

My Time and Place
Perfectly Suit My Needs

$\mathscr{I}$ distinctly remember watching the American pioneers crossing the continent and rejoicing as they endured their difficult tasks and completed their missions. I knew that only those who needed that experience were placed there . . . I sensed that many of us . . . would not have been up to the tasks, that we would have made lousy pioneers . . . Likewise, some of the pioneers . . . could not have endured the trials of today. *Embraced By The Light* - *pages 52-53*

Thine eyes did see my substance, yet being unperfect; and in thy book all my members were written . . . when as yet there was none of them. *Psalms 139:16*

$\mathscr{F}$ather, in creating me and establishing the elements of my life, you acted in perfect knowledge of me and my needs. I thank you humbly for your care. When circumstances in life become difficult to endure or to understand, help me to accept that your wisdom is perfect in all you do, and to trust you have prepared for the difficulties.

Affirmation: **I embrace my time, place and circumstances. They meet my spiritual needs.**

 December 2

Heaven's Vastness Contains Worlds Unnumbered

We are all God's children, and he has filled the immensity of space for us. I traveled tremendous distances, knowing that the stars I saw were not visible from earth. I saw galaxies and traveled to them . . . visiting their worlds and meeting more children of our God, all of them our spiritual brothers and sisters . . . I saw worlds that our most powerful telescopes could never see, and I know the love that exists there. *Embraced By The Light - page 88*

Which alone spreadeth out the heavens, and . . . which maketh Arcturus, Orion, and Pleiades, and . . . which doeth great things past finding out; yea, and wonders without number. Job 9:8-10

The night sky fills me with wonder, my Father. The stars, the planets, the many worlds: all are your beautiful creations and are given in love. Thank you for blessing me with a sense of the vastness and eternal nature of your creation. May I always give you praise and glory.

Affirmation: **I live in gratitude and love for the Creator of this and many worlds.**

 December 3

Sharing My Knowledge
Keeps It Alive

When you receive love or knowledge, you pass it on, and thereby leave yourself open to receive again. If you hold on to it, you don't leave room to receive; you don't need it, because you don't use it . . . Knowledge without revelation is dead; knowledge held on to goes nowhere and helps no one. But the knowledge that we reveal to others takes on a life of its own, and allows us to receive more knowledge to share. *The Awakening Heart - pages 206-207*

Neither do men light a candle, and put it under a bushel, but on a candlestick; and it giveth light unto all that are in the house. Matthew 5:15

Thank you, Father, for showing me that, as I give, so I receive. Bless me to use and to teach the truths I have learned of you generously and with love. I want to be worthy to learn so much more. Keep my knowledge of you alive in me.

Affirmation: **By all my actions I manifest my knowledge and love of God.**

December 4

When I Am Ready, Windows of Opportunity Appear

$\mathcal{G}$od began to prepare me for the windows of opportunity to exercise my will, and while I knew those same windows could come around more than once, I knew, too, that I had to stay in tune with him to recognize the golden opportunity the first time it came around, the golden moment when the window was open. *The Awakening Heart - page 38*

That the Lord thy God may shew us the way wherein we may walk, and the thing that we may do.
Jeremiah 42:3

Father, bless me with daily courage to seize the moments of opportunity that come to me. Help me to trust in your wisdom and in the spirit that encourages me to act in the interest of growth and in spreading your ripples of love.

Affirmation: **I recognize possibilities and trust the ways of the Lord.**

I Deserve My Best Efforts, Regardless of Past Failures

We deserve our best efforts, regardless of past failures. We deserve to forgive ourselves, even as we forgive those who may have damaged us. Too many of us punish ourselves and others for mistakes that God has already forgiven. *The Ripple Effect - page 155*

To the Lord our God belong mercies and forgivenesses, though we have rebelled against him . . . Daniel 9:9

Father, bless me to show a repentant heart, and bless me with faith in your forgiveness. In spite of my downfalls, I want to move forward with honor and moral strength. But I need the peace of your forgiveness so that I can forgive myself. Assure me, Father, that you do forgive me. And help me accept my frailties, understanding what I must learn from them and how they help me grow. Thank you for your love and forgiveness, Father.

Affirmation: **I forgive myself just as God promises his unconditional love and forgiveness.**

My Awakened Heart Comes Closer to God

Allowing our goodness to ripple into the lives of others will not only bring us closer to the divine, it will create the spiritual Awakening of the world. This Awakening is now gathering momentum, leading many to come closer to God. This movement is universal and unstoppable. And it must proceed from our hearts, our lives, into the lives of others. It is not God's gracious work alone; it is our work, our opportunity, and it can only progress as we let our lights shine. *The Ripple Effect - page xvii*

Awake, awake; put on thy strength, O Zion; put on thy beautiful garments . . . Isaiah 52:1

Father, thank you for placing in my heart the desire to open myself to you and to your spirit. I will show gratitude by sharing my new and joyful inner life with others. I will help in your great work of awakening people to the reality of you and of their own divine nature.

Affirmation: **I gladly give my heart and hands to the beautiful unfolding of spirit across the world.**

December 7

The Godliness Within
Accepts Me as I Am

We are part of God. We are made from his love. The purity within us is striving to get out, and will get out if we will stop fearing our weaknesses, hating our enemies, and feasting on negativity. We can accept who we are—the good and the bad—and we can forgive all who hurt us. *The Ripple Effect - page 156*

According as his divine power hath given unto us all things that pertain unto life and godliness, through the knowledge of him that hath called us to glory and virtue: 2 Peter 1:3

Father, strengthen me to more perfectly follow the example and teachings of Jesus. Help me to love without condition, and to use the power of that love to overcome every obstacle before me. For I know if I do, I will feel and nourish the divine inside of me.

Affirmation: **I am called to express divine love in myself and to encourage the expression of it in others.**

Personal Sacrifice Teaches Unconditional Love

Life on earth is our opportunity to learn unconditional love as Jesus taught it, to serve and sacrifice personal welfare in behalf of others. Part of Jesus' mission was to die for us . . . ours is to live as he did. *The Ripple Effect - page 31*

Hereby perceive we the love of God, because he laid down his life for us: and we ought to lay down our lives for the brethren. 1 John 3:16

Father, my life can be hectic, and my schedule, full. Help me to make time for serving others, for volunteering my talents, for lending a hand to someone in need. Bless me with greater capacity to sacrifice, to place the needs of others above my own. Teach me to live within this world as Jesus would. Thank you, Father.

Affirmation: **I freely give my life in service, as Jesus did.**

I Have an Inner Witness of Christ

We need not fear meeting Jesus Christ. Our spirits already know him, and when we meet him again, we will regain that knowledge. Even today our inner voice will speak of him if we open ourselves and listen. *The Ripple Effect - page 112*

And they shall not teach every man his neighbor, and every man his brother, saying, Know the Lord: for all shall know me, from the least to the greatest. Hebrews 8:11

Father, thank you for the whisperings of the Spirit that testify of your Son Jesus Christ. Bless me as my spirit grows in that knowledge, and help me to stay receptive to the Spirit and to the confirmation of truth that already exists in my heart.

Affirmation: **I have an inner witness of Jesus Christ and his sacrifice for me.**

December 10

Knowledge + Experience = Understanding and Wisdom

*A*ll experience is for our good, and sometimes it takes what we would consider negative experience to help develop our spirits. We were very willing, even anxious, as spirits to accept all of our ailments, illnesses, and accidents here to help better ourselves spiritually. I understood that in the spirit world our earth time is meaningless. The pain we experience on earth is for just a moment, just a split second of consciousness in the spirit world, and we are very willing to endure it. *Embraced By The Light - page 67*

*W*e glory in tribulations also: knowing that tribulation worketh patience; And patience, experience; and experience, hope . . . *Romans 5:3-4*

*F*ather, I am grateful for each step I take towards wisdom. I know that life can produce many hardships and pain, but I am willing to face these knowing they are truly short-lived and for a higher purpose. Bless me with endurance and faith to keep me spiritually minded and righteously directed.

Affirmation: **My spirit accepts all challenges as instrumental to my higher development.**

December 11

The Power of My Prayers
Ripples on into Heaven

We will never know all the effects of our prayers in this life. We won't know all the good we do, the hearts we touch, the lives we bless. We will not even know what good we have brought into our own lives through prayer. And we cannot know—until we get there—what joy we give heaven by the power of our prayers. *The Ripple Effect - page 107*

The prayer of the upright is [the Lord's] delight. Proverbs 15:8

Father, how wonderful it is to come to you in prayer and to express what is in my heart. These moments with you soothe me and bless me richly by bringing to focus what is important in my life. Bless me to share with others the wonders of communicating with you to help them know that praying is simply voicing our heart's inner desires. Thank you, Father, for conversing with us, your children, and for giving us a direct way to talk one-on-one with you.

Affirmation: **I pray to invite God into my life and to request his blessings for others.**

December 12

Continual Prayer Keeps Me in God's Presence

*A*ny form of prayer is a personal moment in the presence of God. Verbal prayer is often the most powerful, but prayer can be silent, too. It can be a formal offering at preset times, or it can evolve into a constant state of being, continual meditation that communicates with God at all hours. *The Ripple Effect - page 95*

I will bless the Lord at all times: his praise shall continually be in my mouth. Psalms 34:1

Thank you, Father. I treasure my intimate and personal moments in your presence. You are always available to me in your love. Bless me to make an attitude of prayer my constant state of being so that I will experience your continuous love.

Affirmation: **I seek daily, personal moments in the presence of God.**

December 13

Jesus' Love for Me
Never Waivers or Fails

*A*s I remained in the Savior's glow, in his absolute love, I realized that when I had feared him as a child I had actually moved myself further from him. When I thought he didn't love me, I was moving my love from him. He never moved. I saw now that he was like a sun in my galaxy. I moved all around him, sometimes nearer and sometimes farther away, but his love never failed. *Embraced By The Light - page 60*

*A*ll that the Father giveth me shall come to me; and him that cometh to me I will in no wise cast out. *John 6:37*

*F*ather, thank you for sending your Son Jesus to bring to the world your unconditional love. Through your example in him, he has blessed us with love that never waivers or fails. Bless me with assurance that I am always loved. May I never let anything come into my life that would draw me away from being near him.

*A*ffirmation: **I rely upon Jesus' love. No matter what I think or what I do, his love for me never waivers.**

December 14

Opposition Strengthens
My Ability to Love

*W*ithout an opposing energy, our power to love would never be strengthened sufficiently to allow us to progress in the eternities. Satan is the spiritual personification of opposition, as he stands in opposition to the Kingdom of God—to all that is good . . . Without him, there would be no battle, no victory, no gain.
The Ripple Effect - page 82

*B*ehold, I have created the smith that bloweth the coals in the fire, and that bringeth forth an instrument for his work; and I have created the waster to destroy.
Isaiah 54:16

*F*ather, you have created this world as a place where good and evil may play against each other so that, by experience, we may learn. How wise and broad is your wisdom to have created also a Tempter to aid your children in their growth. Nevertheless, Father, when the time comes for testing, hold me in the shelter of your arms.

Affirmation: **My love is strong enough to withstand all challenges before me.**

My Thirst for Righteousness Draws Me to God

My interests had changed, and I was painfully aware that my life before had been very shallow. I had a new interest now, an unquenchable thirst for great spiritual knowledge . . . *The Awakening Heart - page 23*

Blessed are they which do hunger and thirst after righteousness . . . Matthew 5:6

Father, bless my mind and spirit to yearn for that knowledge which leads me to you and to your will for me. Encourage me to pursue the treasures of the Spirit and not the interests of the world. May I continuously desire to learn of you and to wear the mantle of love that causes me to make your will my own.

Affirmation: **I feed my soul's yearning for God. I search out his truths and righteousness.**

Angels Have Charge over Me

I saw that many of my experiences had been orchestrated by guardian angels. Some experiences were sad and some were joyful, but all were calculated to bring me to higher levels of knowledge. I saw that the guardian angels remained with me through my trials, helping me in any way they could. Sometimes I had many guardian angels around me, sometimes just a few, depending on my needs. *Embraced By The Light - page 115*

For he shall give his angels charge over thee, to keep thee in all thy ways. They shall bear thee up in their hands, lest thou dash thy foot against a stone. *Psalms 91:11-12*

Father, thank you for your tenderness and love in directing angels to watch over your children and to prepare the way ahead for their growth. Bless me with wisdom to see in the unexpected your higher purposes at work.

Affirmation: **God blesses me with angels to attend me in my need.**

Loving Myself Allows God to Flow Through Me

Loving ourselves does not mean to grow in ego. Rather it means to find greater humility as we recognize our weaknesses and our absolute dependence upon our Creator. Self-love is allowing God to flow through us. It is respect for our own divinity. It is learning to accept who we are with all our perfections and imperfections. *The Ripple Effect - page 154*

Charity suffereth long, and is kind; charity envieth not; charity vaunteth not itself, is not puffed up. Doth not behave itself unseemly, seeketh not her own, is not easily provoked, thinketh no evil . . . 1 Corinthians 13:4-6

Thank you, Father. I can love myself because you created me worthy of love. Help me to be true to my spirit and to who I really am. Teach me to grow to my highest potential, and to see myself as divine.

Affirmation: **I honor my divinity by respecting and loving my higher self.**

My Beliefs Radiate in My Countenance

When we trust in God, he guides and directs us to further knowledge as we need it. Growth is a process, and when we take time to internalize and understand what we believe, we are more richly blessed; our beliefs radiate in our countenances for all to see. All I needed to do was to share freely what had been given to me and to set the best example of love I could. *The Awakening Heart - pages 43-44*

Ye shine as lights in the world; Holding forth the word of life . . . Philippians 2:15-16

Father, when my growth seems slow, help me to understand that everything has its perfect timing. Bless me not to become complacent but to continue searching for truth, trusting in you for the process of understanding it. May your truths sink deep within me, and radiate outward to influence others.

Affirmation: **I ponder God's truths and internalize them. They are a part of my essence.**

December 19

Angels Seek Good Will for All God's Children

I saw that we could literally call down thousands of angels in our aid if we ask in faith. I saw that we are all equal in their eyes, great or small, talented or handicapped, leaders or followers, saints or sinners. We are all precious and carefully watched over. Their love never fails us. *Embraced By The Light - page 121*

And suddenly there was with the angel a multitude of the heavenly host praising God, and saying . . . on earth peace, good will toward men. *Luke 2:13-14*

Father, I rest secure in knowing that you are mindful of my needs and desires. Thank you for directing hosts of angels to watch over and protect me from that which lies outside your will. When times are most difficult, bless me with greater confidence that angels are near with their loving, gentle spirits, lending me energy and encouragement.

Affirmation: **Loving, caring angels surround and protect every aspect of my life.**

December 20

My Faith Through Prayer
Heals Those I love

By prayer the dead have been raised and the sick have been healed. More importantly, broken spirits have been lifted and healed.
The Ripple Effect - page 104

And the prayer of faith shall save the sick, and the Lord shall raise him up . . . James 5:15

Father, thank you for the healing miracles you have given me and my loved ones in answer to prayer. Knowing that your love is all-powerful, gives me the peace and comfort of knowing I can turn to you in all my needs. Bless those who live without this comfort and faith to know that your love is with them. Touch every heart with the wonder and power of your healing love. I am grateful to know that through my prayers of faith, and because of your desire and power to save, all things can be done.

Affirmation: **I pray earnestly from my heart for those in need. I know my Lord hears and answers prayers.**

December 21

In Searching for God
I Find Him in Me

The more difficult part of my search for God's presence was to find him in me, so that I would be ready to serve him on a moment's notice if need be. *The Awakening Heart - page 38*

Abide in me, and I in you. As the branch cannot bear fruit of itself, except it abide in the vine; no more can ye, except ye abide in me . . . He that abideth in me, and I in him, the same bringeth forth much fruit: for without me ye can do nothing. John 15:4

Father, thank you for blessing me with your incredible Spirit which lets me share in your wisdom, power and love. Its influence makes me desire to serve you in greater ways. And my heart is more willing to serve others thorough your divine direction. Make me always aware of your Spirit residing within me, of your nearness as my faithful loving Father. May I see all those whom I serve as your precious children who are worthy of great sacrifice.

Affirmation: **I acknowledge God in myself and in those I serve. We are His beloved children.**

December 22

My Spirit Knows the Language of the Almighty God

Since there is no language in the spirit world that we are familiar with on earth, the knowledge that is given there can only be given to the spirit. *The Awakening Heart - page 206*

There is a spirit in man: and the inspiration of the Almighty giveth them understanding. Job 32:8

Thank you, Father, for blessing my spirit to communicate directly with you. Bless me to hear clearly when my spirit relays your word to my mind and heart. And help me to step outside my ego when interpreting your word, so that your meaning and intent come through pure and true. Bless me to trust the "knowing" deep in my soul over anything else which attempts to influence me.

Affirmation: **I delight in my spirit's familiarity with my Creator . He communicates with my Soul.**

Heavenly Tones in Music
Comfort and Mend My Spirit

I entered the vastness of space and . . . I heard a soft, pleasant sound, a distant but comforting sound that made me happy. It was a tone, similar to a note of music, but was universal and seemed to fill all the space around me. It was followed by another tone at a different pitch, and soon I noticed something of a melody——a vast, cosmic song that soothed and comforted me. The tones produced soft vibrations, and as they touched me I knew that they possessed the power to heal . . . they were like spiritual salve, expressions of love that mended broken spirits. *Embraced By The Light - page 87*

Blessed is the people that know the joyful sound: they shall walk, O Lord, in the light of thy countenance. Psalms 89:15

Bless me, Father, to be more aware of the effect music and sound have on my spirit. Lead me to choose that which heals and uplifts so that I will feel in harmony with your beautiful spirit.

Affirmation: **I choose music which brings solace and beauty and positive energy to my soul.**

Christ Jesus Is the Light of My Life

*H*eaven in all its glory could be summed up in one word: Christ. He is the light of creation, the joy of all life, and above all, the deepest love of our souls. To embrace him is to embrace the meaning of life and the eternal power of God. *The Ripple Effect - page 12*

*T*hen spake Jesus again unto them, saying, I am the light of the world: he that followeth me shall not walk in darkness, but shall have the light of life. *John 8:12*

*F*ather, the presence of Christ empowers my life and makes serving you in righteousness possible. Make me, like him, a light to the world, as I follow in his footsteps and avoid darkness. Bless me to hold Jesus and his redeeming sacrifice sacred, while turning to you, Father, for my eternal source of power.

Affirmation: **Christ, the light and joy of my life, fills me with the eternal power of God.**

God's Perfect Plan
Makes Me Joyful

Upon receiving the plan of creation, we sang in rejoicing and were filled with God's love. We were filled with joy as we saw the growth we would have here on earth and the joyous bonds we would create with each other. Then we watched as the earth was created. We watched as our spirit brothers and sisters entered physical bodies for their turns upon the earth . . . *Embraced By The Light - page 52*

Thus saith God the Lord, he that created the heavens, and stretched them out; he that spread forth the earth, and that which cometh out of it; he that giveth breath unto the people upon it, and spirit to them that walk therein . . . Isaiah 42:5

Open my eyes, Father, to see the true spirits in those I fellowship with daily. May I always be willing to give a helping hand to my brothers and sisters who need me. Bless us all with experiences which will help in our heavenly progression.

Affirmation: **Knowing God's perfect plan, I feel kinship and joy for all my brothers and sisters.**

December 26

In Body and Spirit
I Seek to Glorify God

*O*ur minds, in the cognitive, material world, make decisions for our souls. The war between these two forces can be intense; the spirit or "emotional" part of us choosing one direction, the flesh or "thinking" part often choosing another. The question of life is always the same: which will win, the spirit or the flesh? *The Ripple Effect - page 73*

*G*lorify God in your body, and in your spirit, which are God's. *1 Corinthians 6:20*

*F*ather, thank you for this body which allows my soul to exercise freedom of choice in this world. While I am discovering life in the flesh, bless me with wisdom and courage to choose always that which protects and ensures continued life, and which preserves the purity of my spirit. Most of all, thank you, Father, for creating me and loving me as I am.

Affirmation: **I cherish the divine element of my being, and honor my Creator's path of purity.**

December 27

God, in Spirit, Is the Purest Form of Love

God is love in its purest form. His love seeks nothing from us and demands nothing of us. His love is unconditionally given to all who believe in him. To be in his presence and share his love, we must become as he is and learn to love without judgments and conditions. *The Awakening Heart - page 39*

For I am persuaded, that neither death, nor life, nor angels, nor principalities, nor powers, nor things present, nor things to come, Nor height, nor depth, nor any other creature, shall be able to separate us from the love of God, which is in Christ Jesus our Lord. Romans 8:38-39

Father, your endless, unconditional love permits nothing to separate me from you, even at death. Thank you! My future with you is assured by your grace and forgiveness. Bless me to grow in faith, even unto knowing that I am worthy of your presence and your love. Inspire me to seek every opportunity for growth which will develop in me that same Spirit of love.

Affirmation: **I am created in the image of God who is the purest form of love.**

December 28

This World Offers the Blessings of Spiritual Education

A time was established for each of us to complete our earthly education. Some spirits would come only to be born, to give experience to others and then pass quickly out of this world. Some would live to an old age to complete their goals and benefit others by allowing them opportunities to serve. Some would come . . . and the purpose for their coming would be to provide situations and relationships that would allow us to learn to love. *Embraced By The Light - page 96*

*H*ath not God chosen the poor of this world rich in faith, and heirs of the kingdom which he hath promised to them that love him? *James 2:5-6*

*F*ather, I am grateful for my station in life and for the time given me to serve you. Bless me to live satisfied within the conditions of my life, to desire greater things but not to covet the blessings of others. Your knowledge of us determines which blessings best fit for your purposes. Thank you, Father.

Affirmation: **My time and mission is established by God, who has chosen me.**

December 29

God Blesses My Life with Miracles, Seen and Unseen

Sometimes God will give us a miracle just to remind us that he can. He wants us all to know that we are his children and that his love is there for us . . . For those of us who still doubt his existence and awesome power, God offers all of the evidence of his love and his glory that we need—at times, in the form of miracles. *The Awakening Heart - pages 194-195*

He therefore that ministereth to you the Spirit, and worketh miracles among you, doeth he it by the works of the law, or by the hearing of faith? Galatians 3:5

Father, thank you for miracles in my life that make me aware of greater possibilities through my faith in you. Help me to notice and appreciate even the very smallest of miracles, to find joy and delight in each one.

Affirmation: **My faith in God brings abundant miracles into my life, and I see them more clearly each day.**

My Greatest Gift of Spirit
Is Eternal Life

And when our journey is through, and we too slip from this mortal state to see and hear and feel for ourselves the truths of eternity, we will know for certain that our lives were perfect expressions of our identities, that the things we suffered were perfectly matched to our needs, and that life in mortality—that most mysterious and marvelous gift—was exactly what we needed for our eternal development. *The Ripple Effect - pages 231-232*

And the heavens shall praise thy wonders, O Lord . . . Psalms 89:5

Father, sometimes I wish I knew why I am as I am and why my life is what it is. But knowing would rob me of the growth which comes from discovering by experience what I am made of and what I am meant to become. I look to you, and hold on to your love, and I keep moving by faith, knowing that someday the glorious truth of being mortal will be shown.

Affirmation: **My life is a marvelous gift and is exactly what I need for my eternal growth with God, my Creator.**

 December 31

Index

through, 4/17; Jesus Christ's, 1/11, 2/4, 2/22, 3/11, 3/26, 4/3, 4/22, 4/24, 5/27, 7/17, 8/22, 9/8, 9/21, 11/25, 12/9

experience(s). *See* life experience(s)

failure: cycle of, 7/31; moving on in spite of, 8/17, 12/6; part of the plan, 6/14

faith: acquiring, a reason for being, 8/26; blessings follow trials of, 6/28; brings miracles, 12/30; follows knowledge, 5/28, 7/19; governed by the spirit, 11/11; grows through prayer, 2/2, 3/5; grows through practice, 3/9, 7/19, 11/11; grows through visualizing, 2/11; increases by trials, 1/10, 9/27; in God, 3/14, 4/2, 5/28, 9/12, 10/6; in God's forgiveness, 5/18; is action, 6/27, 9/20; moves mountains, 3/14; moving forward in life through, 9/20, 11/11; overcoming anxiety and fear through, 2/26, 3/3, 4/2, 9/20; power in prayers of, 1/14, 1/17, 10/29, 12/21; seeds of, 3/9; testing limits of, 3/3, 9/27; when God's purposes remain hidden, 3/6, 7/20, 9/12; when lacking knowledge, 3/7

family, departed (*see also* spirit beings): communication with, in dreams, 10/8; know our welfare, 5/1; live on, 5/1; love us still, 5/1; nearness of, 5/7; prayers benefit, 5/29

family, earthly: eternal bonds of, 1/26, 5/1, 5/5, 7/30, 11/5, 12/26; establishing love in, 5/26,

7/3; important to our growth, 2/13, 5/8; provides needed genetic coding, 1/26; sacrifices of, for us, 1/23

fear: attracts its likeness, 11/26; God helps us identify our, 11/8; hinders blessings, 3/12; hinders growth, 2/23, 3/3; hinders love, 5/10, 8/2; love casts out, 8/2; not of God, 4/2; of death, 2/23, 6/17; of life, 4/2, 9/20; of others, 6/29; of trials, 3/27; of weakness, 12/8; overcoming, 3/3, 4/9, 5/10; Satan's greatest tool, 7/16, 8/2; spirit of, 1/2, 4/2

fellowship: in changing the world, 10/7; in prayer, 1/25, 7/5; in sustaining each other, 11/7

flesh (*see also* body): appetites binds us to, 4/26; finding harmony with spirit, 6/5, 7/21, 11/29; houses the spirit or soul, 6/5, 12/27; overcoming the, 1/12, 1/18, 6/5; power in, to express love, 3/30; persistence of, 6/5; spirit governs the, 1/3, 5/11, 6/25; weaker than spirit, 6/5

flexibility (*see also* change): 2/14, 8/10

force (*see also* free will): God never uses, 4/23, 11/30; in changing religious beliefs of others, 4/17, 7/26; nonexistent in heaven, 7/29

forgiveness: before prayer, 5/9; brings healing, 11/4; from God (*see also* God's mercy), 3/7, 5/12, 5/18, 6/2, 8/7, 10/28; give, in order to receive, 10/16; God's patience in, 5/23; in ad-